Lenin's Brain

Lenin's Brain
and Other Tales
from the Secret Soviet Archives

by PAUL R. GREGORY

HOOVER INSTITUTION PRESS
STANFORD UNIVERSITY · STANFORD, CALIFORNIA

www.hoover.org

Hoover Institution Press Publication No. 555

First printing, 2008
14 13 12 11 10 09 08   9 8 7 6 5 4 3 2 1

Set in Celeste and Meta Plus with Senator display by Graphic Composition, Inc.
Manufactured in the United States of America.

The paper used in this publication meets the minimum requirements of the American National Standard for Information Sciences—Permanence of Paper for Printed Library Materials, ANSI Z39.48-1992.

Illustrations are from the collections of the Hoover Institution Archives.
All rights reserved. Please see page 155 for illustration source notes.

Library of Congress Cataloging-in-Publication Data

Gregory, Paul R.
    Lenin's brain and other tales from the secret Soviet archives / by Paul R. Gregory.
        p.   cm. — (Hoover Institution Press publication series ; 555)
    Includes bibliographical references and index.
    ISBN 978-0-8179-4811-5 (cloth : alk. paper) — ISBN 978-0-8179-4812-2 (pbk : alk. paper)
    1. Soviet Union—History—Anecdotes. I. Title.
    DK266.3.G74 2008
    947.084—dc22   2007007691

Dedicated to

Robert Conquest,

a true pioneer,

on his ninetieth birthday.

Contents

List of Illustrations

Foreword

THE HOOVER INSTITUTION ON WAR, REVOLUTION AND PEACE rests on its two pillars of scholarship and archival collections. Hoover scholars address the major political, economic, and social issues of our new century, and Hoover archives offer unique information for scholars seeking to make sense of the past as well as of contemporary times. Our archives contain more than five thousand separate collections covering the entire range of twentieth-century world history and politics, and house the world's richest collection on the history of communism and, particularly, its Russian variant.

This book is a sampling of tales, written by Hoover fellow Paul Gregory, drawn from our collections of Soviet state and party archives. Hoover has played a pioneering role in sponsoring documentary publications (such as the prize-winning, seven-volume *History of Stalin's Gulag*) and in microfilming collections, such as the Communist Party on Trial, the archives of the Central Committee of the Communist Party, and the Gulag administration, to name only three examples. Over the past decade, hundreds of researchers from around the globe (including from Russia) have studied Russia's political, social, and economic history through the prism of these archives.

Only in the past two decades are there more democracies than totalitarian regimes, but the balance is continually shifting. The existence of the Soviet state and party archives makes the Soviet Union, particularly in its most brutal form under Stalin, history's best-documented dictatorship. Stalin's Russia provided the model for China, Cuba, North Korea, and Eastern Europe after World War II. One of the most enthusiastic students of Stalin was none other than Saddam Hussein. To understand the inner workings of dictatorships, Soviet Russia represents a good case study.

Over the past seven years, Paul Gregory has headed our initiative to bring together the two pillars of research and archives through his own research on Soviet history, including his "team" of economists, historians, and political scientists working in our Soviet archives. Their work has brought forth more than forty articles, six books, and two documentary collections, two of which have won international awards. Topics studied include the Gulag, high-level decision making, corruption, the role of the Communist Party, and repression and terror.

All valuable archives are full of stories that either go unnoticed or are buried in the specialized literature. Paul Gregory has selected fourteen tales, some horrific, some puzzling, and others simply entertaining to provide an inside look at how the Soviet dictatorship worked—how to go to war (Afghanistan), how and why to execute or imprison more than a million of its own citizens (the Great Terror), how to honor its saints (the story of Lenin's brain), how to discourage disagreement (Bolshevik discourse), why intellectuals are dangerous (The Ship of Philosophers), and how to dehumanize enemies. It is satisfying to note that these fourteen short stories, taken together, produce a surprising deep understanding of totalitarianism.

A persistent theme of these tales is the relationship between dictatorship and repression, and the need for a special agency (called at various times the OGPU, NKVD, MVD, or KGB) to impose terror on citizens. The archives of these special "organs" were the closest-held secrets of the Soviet Union and they have achieved a new significance in understanding a modern Russian state headed by former officers of such "organs." The reader will note that the "organs" play a role in virtually every story, reflecting their pervasive influence on Soviet life.

Finally, I would say it is only fitting that this book is dedicated to Hoover's own Robert Conquest on his ninetieth birthday. It was Robert Conquest who first penetrated Stalin's Terror, his secret police, and the great famine of the early 1930s using published sources and his remarkable scholarship and intuition. This book is a small but appropriate tribute to his voluminous contributions.

John Raisian
The Tad and Dianne Taube Director,
Hoover Institution on War, Revolution and Peace

Acknowledgments

I WOULD LIKE TO THANK John Raisian (Director of the Hoover Institution) and Richard Sousa (Deputy Director) for their encouragement and support of this undertaking. More generally, I would like to thank the Hoover Institution as a whole for its longstanding commitment to excellence in archival collections. Among the many dedicated archivists at Hoover who provided assistance, I would especially like to thank Carol Leadenham and Lora Soroka.

Lenin's Brain

Chapter One

"Scurrilous Provocation"

The Katyn Massacre[1]

Background:

In a forty-day period starting April 3, 1940, special troops of the Soviet NKVD under the command of "commissar general" Lavrenty Beria systematically executed some twenty-two thousand Poles held in occupied territory and in western provinces of Belorussia and Ukraine. Of these, 4,421 were shot in the Katyn forest, a short distance from the city of Smolensk. The rest were from other camps with exotic names like Starobelskii or Ostashkovskii, but "Katyn" became the symbol of the 1940 Soviet massacre of Polish officers, held in Soviet POW camps.

As a typical NKVD operation, the killings were done in great secrecy. They required a month to carry out because necessary orders had to be distributed to the various camps, victims had to be processed by NKVD tribunals, executioners assembled, and prisoners transported to killing fields. Lacking the sophisticated mass killing machinery of the Nazis, victims were shot one by one before open trenches.

The official Soviet cover story was that there were indeed massacres of Poles in occupied Polish and Soviet territories, but they were carried out by Hitler's SS about one year later. According to the Soviet version, the victims were captured Polish officers assembled into work brigades before their extermination by the Nazis.

Photograph of site of Katyn massacre, located in the vicinity of Smolensk.

As invading German forces occupied these execution sites, they conducted investigations in which they invited the Polish Red Cross to participate. A German commission interviewed eyewitnesses and exhumed bodies that bore the distinctive markings of NKVD executions. Seeing Katyn as a potential wedge between the Soviet Union and the Polish exile government, Nazi propaganda czar Joseph Goebbels released their findings, implicating Stalin's forces in these atrocities. Goebbels' convincing forensic and other evidence indeed caused a deep rift in Soviet-Polish relations, to the great concern of the Allied forces.

After the German retreat and Soviet reoccupation of its western provinces, the Soviet Union began its own investigation. The Burdenko Commission (named after its head, the president of the USSR Academy of Sciences) conveniently concluded that the Germans had massacred the Polish officers in 1941. The Burdenko Commission's findings became the official Soviet mantra and even found support in the Nuremburg trials, in which Nazi Germany was accused of ethnic cleansing of Poles.

The war ended with two competing versions of the mass burial grounds of Poles executed in occupied Polish territories and in the western parts of Ukraine and Belorussia: the German account released by Hitler's chief propagandist, the originator of the "big lie," versus the Soviet account issued by its chief scientist in the name of a heroic wartime ally. It was the Soviet account that was false.

The Soviet state and party archives chronicle a cover-up that began with Stalin's March 5, 1940, top-secret execution order and ended a half century later on January 22, 1991, with an official communication to the Polish ambassador, admitting that NKVD chief Lavrenty Beria was responsible for the killings. The Communist Party's secret files on the Katyn case include fifty-two pages of official documents. They begin with Beria's proposal to execute the Polish prisoners en masse and the Politburo's (Stalin's) written execution order. The Katyn file then turns to the increasingly shaky cover-up and pressure from Polish "friends" to come clean with the true story.

Throughout most of the fifty-year cover-up, the Katyn affair lay dormant. Soviet leaders from Nikita Khrushchev, to Leonid Brezhnev, to Mikhail Gorbachev—all of whom knew the true story—probably breathed sighs of relief during periods of quiet, hoping the matter was dead and buried. Dormant periods were followed by periodic bursts of indignant propaganda as Western interest in Katyn was revived by television reports, the release of new books, or pressure from indignant Polish relatives. The Soviet official account eventually fell victim to Gorbachev's need to defend the "friendly" regime of General Jaruszelski from attacks by opposition parties. The Katyn "problem" finally drove a reluctant Gorbachev to a grudging and vague admission of guilt based, of course, on "newly discovered evidence."

There are no Soviet heroes in the Katyn files. The head of the USSR Academy of Sciences falsified scientific evidence. Khrushchev, the leader who disclosed Stalin's crimes, concealed the documents as a potential source of embarrassment. The reformer Gorbachev tried every possible maneuver to avoid telling the Poles the truth, and even then gave a "confession" that protected Stalin and the Politburo of the Communist Party.

The Files: The Smoking Gun

In September of 1939, Germany invaded Poland from the west and the USSR invaded from the east in the wake of the Molotov-Ribbentrop Pact. More than one hundred thousand Polish prisoners, mostly soldiers but also civilian officials, were captured and interned in occupied territory and in western provinces of Belorussia and Ukraine. Upon capture, they did not know their extreme danger. They hoped to be treated as normal POWs.

Two years earlier, Stalin began his "national operations" against ethnic Germans, Latvians, Koreans, Lithuanians, and other minorities working in strategic industries or located in border areas. Stalin feared that the multi-ethnic Soviet Union was a breeding ground for fifth-columnists, who would aid the enemy in case of war. Among his least favored ethnic minorities were Poles, the subject of Stalin's second national operations decree of August 9, 1937, which ordered the imprisonment or execution of members of underground Polish military organizations, political immigrants, and "anti-Soviet nationalistic elements."

For Stalin, the concentration of Polish officers and civilian officials in his own POW camps offered a tempting opportunity to wipe out another potential source of enemy support using the most reliable method—execution. Moreover, he had a highly efficient ally in charge of his NKVD, who knew how to carry out such operations and to keep them quiet. Lavrenty Beria, the head of the NKVD since November of 1938, was already in charge of the national operations being conducted in the Soviet borderlands. He understood well what his boss wanted and was only too ready to come up with suitable proposals.

The Katyn smoking gun is not hard to find. The most important decisions of the Soviet Union were made formally by its highest ruling body, the Politburo, which in 1940 was a puppet of Stalin. A decision as important as the execution of thousands of Polish POWS would have had to emanate from the Politburo.

Politburo "meetings" (often there were no meetings; rather, members were asked to vote in writing or by telephone) dealt with "questions" posed by various agencies of government, such as the justice ministry, the industrial ministries, or Beria's NKVD. Such "questions" were posted in the form of written proposals or draft decrees and were approved either in the Politburo meeting or by circulating the question to various Politburo members for their signatures. The Politburo's (Stalin's) execution order for Polish officers, therefore, had to be present among Politburo documents.

True to expectations, the Katyn file shows that, on March 5, 1940, Beria addressed a "question of the NKVD" to Stalin, informing him that 14,736 Polish "officers, officials, police officials, gendarmes, and prison officials" were being held in camps in occupied Polish territory and 18,632 similar persons were being held in camps in the western provinces of Ukraine and Belorussia. Beria's "question" was to the point: "Taking as true the fact that all of them are hardened and unredeemable enemies of Soviet power, the NKVD recommends that their cases be examined in special order with the application of the highest measure of punishment—shooting." The case reviews should be done "without summoning the arrested parties and without the posting of charges." In effect, Beria's "question" was for approval to summarily execute as many as 34,000 Polish prisoners of war. A note on Beria's memo, handwritten by some faceless bureaucrat, listed his proposal as the "second question of the NKVD" on the Politburo's agenda of the same day.

Clearly, Beria did not suddenly come up with this proposal on March 5, 1940, for a Politburo meeting later in the day. Stalin and

Beria met one-on-one regularly in Stalin's private office. This is where they would have agreed to the Katyn massacre. It was Stalin's practice to implicate his fellow Politburo members in such matters, despite their perfunctory participation. The other Politburo members knew the Katyn decision was already taken when they saw Stalin's bold signature scrawled at the top of Beria's "question." The signatures of three other Politburo members (Voroshilov, Molotov, and Mikoian) are also affixed to Beria's proposal. Presumably, they were in the building on that day to sign. Two other Politburo members (Kalinin and Kaganovich) were canvassed by telephone and their positive votes are recorded by someone's hand in the left margin of Beria's memo. The Politburo records show that the question was formally approved as "Question no. 144 of the NKVD" in protocol no. 18 of the Politburo session of March 5, 1940.

The excerpt from the Politburo minutes was directed to Beria, placing the responsibility on the first special department of the NKVD to carry out the executions. The document was labeled top secret, requiring recipients to return their copies within 24 hours. Copies were placed in the top secret "special files" of the Politburo, where they remained for Stalin's successors.

The executions began one month later. Beria was a meticulous planner, and his efficiency improved with each operation. Later in May of 1944, he was to boast to Stalin about one of his most successful operations, carried out in two days: "Today, May 20, the operation of deportation of Crimean Tartars was completed. Exiled and transported in echelons 180,014. Echelons sent to new places of settlement in Uzbek republic. There were no incidents in the course of the operation."[2] The Katyn operation was on a much smaller scale, but it needed care. Special tribunals had to be set up in the various camps; executioners had to be assembled, the victims had to be transported to the place of execution, clerks were needed to prepare the case files and to compile execution statistics. An adequate supply of vodka had to be brought in for those who did the actual shooting. Unlike the Nazis, the NKVD used its own officers as executioners, not ordinary soldiers who were likely to tell their friends and relatives. Above all, strict secrecy had to be maintained.

Beria's efficiency was evident in the Katyn operation. His special

NKVD forces processed and dispatched some 22,000 Polish prisoners between April 3 and May 19, 1940, for an average of over five hundred executions per day. Bodies were buried in covered ditches by special NKVD detachments until discovered by occupying German forces two years later.

The Cover Story

The Katyn affair remained dormant throughout much of the postwar period, although never far below the surface in the "friendly" People's Republic of Poland and in the Polish Diaspora. The top-secret Katyn file was reviewed by Soviet leaders, albeit infrequently. Records show that Nikita Khrushchev was briefed on its contents in 1959. Some top official checked the file out on March 9, 1965. Konstantin Chernenko and KGB head Yury Andropov reviewed the file in April of 1981 and two functionaries show it passing from one department to another on April 18, 1989, under Gorbachev.

Stalin's immediate successor, Nikita Khrushchev, was given the March 5, 1940, execution order and was briefed by his minister of interior, A. Shelepin, in a handwritten memo dated March 20, 1959:

> Accounting records and other materials are preserved by the Committee of State Security dating from 1940 on the execution of imprisoned and interned officers, gendarmes, police officials, land owners etc. persons of the former bourgeois Poland. In all, 21,857 of them were shot by orders of troikas of the NKVD. . . . The entire operation was based on the decree of the Central Committee of March 5, 1940.

Shelepin cynically concluded:

> For Soviet organs, these cases do not represent operational interest, nor are they of historical value. They scarcely represent any real interest for our Polish friends. To the contrary, an accidental revelation could lead to unwelcome consequences for our government. Even more, we have an official version of the Katyn forest executions, confirmed by Soviet organs of power based on the 1944 Special Commission for the Investigation of the Executions of Interned Polish Officers by German-Fascist Occupation

Forces. Based upon the above facts, it would appear wise to destroy all these documents.

Shelepin's attached handwritten decree for the Politburo calling for the "liquidation of all materials carried out in accordance with the Central Committee Decree of March 5, 1940, with the exception of protocols of meetings of the troikas that condemned the prisoners to death" was not adopted, a decision that Khrushchev's successors surely considered a grave mistake. With a submissive Poland firmly entrenched in the Soviet bloc, Khrushchev figured that the March 5, 1940, decree was safe, deep in the vaults of the Politburo.

The next entry in the Katyn file (now referred to as the Katyn "tragedy") came twelve years later, as Khrushchev's successor, Leonid Brezhnev, and his foreign minister, Andrei Gromyko, and KGB head Yury Andropov grappled with the "Anti-Soviet campaign surrounding the Katyn matter." On April 12, 1971, Gromyko warned the Politburo that a book on Katyn and an upcoming BBC film were to blame the Soviet Union for the Katyn massacre. Gromyko's memo recommended informing "our Polish friends" about these unfortunate events.

The BBC film was considered a sufficient threat for the Politburo to move against the British government. Brezhnev's preemptive strike came in the form of secret Politburo instructions to the Soviet ambassador to the UK (with copies to the Soviet embassy in Poland), to protest the upcoming BBC film based on a "scurrilous" book on the "Katyn tragedy" in the following words:

> The English side knows well that Hitler's forces have been proven responsible for this crime by an authoritative special commission, which carried out an investigation of this crime immediately after German occupation forces were driven out of the Smolensk region. In 1945–46, the Nuremburg tribunal pronounced German military criminals guilty of the policy of extermination of the Polish people and, in particular, of the shooting of Polish prisoners of war in the Katyn forest.

The English were also to be told in convoluted diplomatic language: "The taking of a position on this matter by the English government would be in stark contradiction to efforts to improve relations with the Soviet Union." The text of the ambassador's protest was approved by the Politburo on September 8, 1972.

This blunt diplomatic warning to the British government to keep its hands off the Katyn affair bore little fruit; the Politburo was back to fighting anti-Soviet "slander" four years later.

The next Katyn record dates to the Politburo's April 5, 1976, "Measures to combat Western propaganda about the so-called Katyn affair." The Politburo ordered the preparation jointly with the Polish Communist Party of "some kind of official declaration from our side so as not to give the opposing side a chance to use these polemics for anti-Soviet purposes." In addition, the KGB was ordered to use its "unofficial channels" to let ruling circles in Western countries know that "their use of anti-Soviet falsifications would be considered as a provocation intended toward worsening the international situation." The Smolensk party committee, located a few miles from the Katyn site, was given instructions to maintain in good order a memorial to Polish officers. The Politburo decree also repeated the official Soviet version in a secret "short report about the Katyn affair" that Goebbels himself created an "international medical commission" of sympathetic satellite countries to conduct exhumations in 1943 and to produce a false book blaming the Soviets for the purpose of worsening USSR-Polish relations. The true version was that told by the Burdenko Commission: It was Nazi troops that carried out the massacre of Polish officers working in camps in the region.

Leonid Brezhnev died in November of 1982 and was replaced by KGB head Andropov, who was then replaced by Konstantin Chernenko upon his death sixteen months later. Chernenko's rule ended with his death in March of 1985, and he was replaced by the young and "reform minded" Mikhail Gorbachev. Gorbachev embarked two years later on his course of perestroika that loosened Soviet control over its increasingly restive Eastern European satellites. Nowhere was the challenge to Soviet hegemony more acute than in Poland, whose independent labor movement was threatening the "friendly" regime of General Jaruszelski. Soviet stonewalling on Katyn was playing into the hands of the Polish anti-Soviet opposition.

The next official Katyn entry comes in May of 1988 as a different

Politburo, now headed by Gorbachev with Eduard Shevardnadze as his foreign minister, prepared for Gorbachev's visit of friendship to the embattled Jaruzelski. Although the bitter Poles would accept nothing less than a full Soviet admission and apology, the Politburo, in its May 5, 1988, meeting, is shown grasping at straws. To improve relations, the Politburo proposed to build a memorial to the victims of the massacre "destroyed by Hitlerites in Katyn." To make matters worse, the tin-eared Politburo also proposed a memorial to the five hundred Soviet POWs killed at Katyn by the "Hitlerites." The Politburo offered another cosmetic concession: a "simplified procedure" for Poles wishing to visit Katyn.

Gorbachev's visit took place July 11 to 14, 1988, and was followed by a Politburo meeting of September 1, 1988, to "realize the proposals put forward during the official friendship visit of General Secretary Gorbachev to Poland." The one proposal relating to Katyn was to "jointly with the Polish People's Republic declare a competition for the best proposal for a memorial to Polish officers buried in Katyn."

Katyn continued to plague Soviet-Polish relations. Gorbachev's Politburo continued its attempts to placate the Polish side, such as promoting the burial of a symbolic urn of ashes from Katyn in Warsaw.

The first crack in the official Soviet line is a memo from Gorbachev's trusted advisor, the head of the international department of the Central Committee, V. Falin, who sent the following frank assessment to Gorbachev on March 6, 1989:

> We had in mind that a joint commission of Soviet and Polish scholars, created as a result of joint agreements at the highest level, could work out a consensus on Katyn.[3] After one and a half years, however, the Commission cannot even begin discussion because the Soviet scholars are not authorized to cast doubt on the official version. In the meantime the Polish side has introduced evidence about the unfounded argumentation used by the Soviet extraordinary commission of N. Burdenko in its 1944 report.... A year ago, the Soviet side was given a secret report about the participation of the Polish Red Cross in exhumation work in Katyn in April–May 1943 and the conclusion that the NKVD was responsible. Now without waiting for our response, the Polish side is publishing this report in their press.

Falin concluded on a pessimistic note:

> In the whole, the problem will not go away. In case of a further worsening of the internal political situation in Poland, the Katyn issue may be used as an excuse for retribution against the Soviet Union.

A similarly bleak assessment "About the Katyn Issue" co-authored by Falin, Shevardnadze, and KGB deputy director Kriuchkov dated two weeks later (March 22, 1989) concluded:

> In his press declaration, the Polish representative has legalized the official position of the Polish government that the liquidation of the Polish officers was the responsibility of the USSR. It is true that guilt was laid on Stalin's NKVD and not on the Soviet government. The tactics of the Polish government are understandable. It is trying to reduce pressure which has been building because of the unfulfilled promise to clarify the Katyn affair. To a degree the pressure is also on us, because there has been no movement on this issue for two years by the joint commission of scholars. Our analysis of the situation shows that to further drag out this business will turn into a millstone around our necks not only for the past but also for current Soviet-Polish relations. . . . It seems we cannot avoid an explanation to the Polish government and Polish society about these tragic events of the past. Maybe it would be wise to say what really happened and who was concretely responsible and thus close the matter. To take such action in the final analysis would cause less damage than the current course of doing nothing.

As Soviet options shrank, the Politburo, on March 31, 1989, ordered the USSR Procurator, the KGB, and the international and ideological departments of the Central Committee to prepare proposals about the future "Soviet line" on the Katyn affair. The impending state visit of General Jaruszelski at the end of April to Moscow moved Soviet authorities into high gear. A draft decree dated April 22, 1989, called for a final report by August 1, 1989. The main archival administrations were to cooperate by supplying materials, and the state radio, and Pravda and Izvestia were to be ready to report the results of the investigation.

The next entry is a February 23, 1990, secret memo entitled "Further

Information on the Katyn Tragedy" prepared for Gorbachev by the USSR General Procurator (N. S. Trubin). The memo speaks volumes about the so-called 'glasnost' (openness) of the Gorbachev years.

The procurator's memo informs Gorbachev about the work of Soviet historians charged with finding the true story of Katyn. The historians were given access to various "special" Soviet archives but were not given the March 5, 1940, "smoking gun" decree. Nevertheless, they uncovered sufficient evidence to prove Soviet culpability, such as memos from Beria to his deputy setting up the operation, daily prisoner transport records, embargoes on incoming and outgoing mail, and lists of "departing" prisoners that were not forwarded to the center (meaning they were dead). The procurator's key conclusion:

> Soviet archival documents confirm the fate of the interned Polish officers even in the absence of evidence of orders to shoot and bury them. On the basis of these documentary facts, Soviet historians are preparing materials for publication, and several of these will be published in June or July. Such publications place us in a new situation. Our argument that we cannot find archival materials that disclose the truth about Katyn would no longer be believable. The material uncovered by our historians, and they have uncovered only a part of our little secrets, in conjunction with the materials uncovered by the Polish side would scarcely allow us to hold to our earlier version.

The proposal to Gorbachev:

> Communicate to Jaruszelski that as a result of a careful archival review, we have not found direct evidence of orders, directives etc., allowing us to establish the concrete time and guilty parties of the Katyn tragedy. However, in the main archives of the NKVD material has been uncovered that raises doubts about the Burdenko report of 1944. We can conclude that the execution of the Polish officers in the Katyn region was the work of the NKVD and personally Beria and [his deputy] Merkulov [no mention of Stalin!]. There remains the question in what form and when to inform Polish and Soviet societies. For this, we need the advice of the President of the Polish Republic bearing in mind the need to close this matter and at the same time avoid an upheaval of emotions.

Although the house of cards was collapsing, Gorbachev did not rush to admit the "truth" to the Polish side. A sidebar to Gorbachev's presidential directive "About the Results of the Visit of the Polish Foreign Minister" of November 3, 1990, blandly states that the Soviet side will "accelerate research" on the fate of Polish officers held by the Soviets in 1939 "relating to events and facts from the history of Soviet-Polish relations that have damaged both sides."

The long-awaited Soviet "confession" is mentioned in a memo prepared by the General Procurator (N. S. Trubin) in forty-five copies dated January 22, 1991, "About the course of the criminal investigation about the fate of fifteen thousand Polish POWs held in 1939–1940 in NKVD camps." The faded memo is scarcely legible, but it tells that Beria's Directive No. 5866/5 ordered the NKVD's prisoner-of-war division and camp administrations to prepare cases for submission to NKVD tribunals (formed to pronounce death sentences). It also tells that, between April 3 and May 16, 1940, contingents of Polish POWs were dispatched by rail from the various camps where they were held by the NKVD. The report concludes: "Investigation of the matter continues. The USSR General Procurator, considering the importance of these new facts, is periodically informing the Polish side." The memo mentions a meeting (date cannot be read) with the Polish ambassador to brief him on these findings.

Why Not Tell the Truth?

When pressed to the limit, Gorbachev decided on a minimalist version of the truth. Although there was ample proof that Stalin's Politburo had ordered the killings, the "confession" cited only an obscure operational order from Beria. In customary Soviet form, the confession also named a relatively low-level NKVD officer along with Beria as another scapegoat.

Why could not a "reformer" of Gorbachev's ilk bring himself in 1991 (fifty years after the fact) to tell the Poles the full story? There are two answers: One is that the Soviets did not want to admit that the massacre was ordered by the Politburo, even though it was Stalin's Politburo. The signatures on the death warrants were not only Stalin's but other Soviet leaders who played prominent roles during the war and early postwar period. Stalin's practice of implicating his fellow leaders paid off long after his death. Second, the 1944 cover-up (the Burdenko Commission) was also approved by the highest "organs of Soviet power," in which the Soviet leaders of the 1970s and 1980s were already playing leading roles. The executions were the work of Stalin and Beria; the cover-up and its continuation were the work of the second generation of Soviet leaders—the Brezhnevs, Andropovs, Kosygins, and even Gorbachevs—who came to power after Stalin's purges of the old Bolsheviks.

Chapter Two

The Four Faces of Stalin

Background

Stalin was capable of incredible cruelty. He was of medium height; his face was scarred by smallpox; he waddled when he walked; and he continually sucked on his pipe. He had incredible patience; he spoke simply with a strong Georgian accent. He lacked humor and was not known to joke. According to his former secretary, who defected to the West in the 1920s: "He had only one passion, absolute and devouring: lust for power. It was a maniacal passion, that of an Asian satrap of long ago. It occupied him entirely and was the unique goal of his life."[1] Stalin had no close friends; his immediate political associates served as his social circle, at Stalin's beck and call. They were bound to him by fear rather than friendship.

This chapter shows four different faces of Stalin, four different modes of behavior all directed toward his overriding goal of gaining and holding on to absolute power. There is the solicitous, magnanimous, and jocular Stalin. There is the reluctant Stalin, required to do unpleasant things because it is the party's wish. There is the Stalin applying praise and flattery with cynical cruelty. Finally, there is the true Stalin, directly carrying out acts of cruelty without any pangs of morality or remorse.

Stalin at the hunt with his comrades.

Face 1: The Magnanimous Stalin

Stalin knew how to use charm and flattery when necessary. Most of his letters to his deputies were matter of fact, but he would also express concern about their health or their fatigue from hard work and send greetings to their wives ("Greetings from Nadia [Stalin's wife] to Zhemchuzhina [Molotov's wife whom Stalin later arrested]").[2] He composed witty poems "dedicated to [Politburo member] Comrade Kalinin," and invited colleagues to visit him in Sochi [To Sergo Ordzhonikidze: "It is good that you have decided on a vacation. Come to me along the way. I would be very glad."].[3]

Much of Stalin's efforts from the mid-1920s through the early thirties were devoted to keeping Politburo members on his side and settling conflicts among them. Stalin had to work out compromises before personal conflicts threatened his coalition. He also had to keep his policy initiatives—collectivization and industrialization—on target, and he knew that praise of subordinates was a potent motivator. He met regularly with leading officials in his private office. We have no transcripts of such meetings, but we presume Stalin used them to bully or to charm. We can find traces of his charm offensives in his correspondence.

Stalin's use of flattery and praise is evident in a 1939 telegram to the director of Far North Construction (a Comrade K. A. Pavlov)—a Gulag division that employed tens of thousands of prisoners mining precious metals under the harshest of climatic conditions.

In his telegram, Stalin magnanimously chides Pavlov for not nominating himself for a medal of "Labor Valor." He also gives Pavlov the privilege to decide himself whom to award medals among his managers and workers, including prisoners.

Ciphered Telegram of I.V. Stalin to K.A. Pavlov [Director of Far North Construction, Dal'stroi] *concerning the rewarding of workers, January 24, 1939.*[4]

Magadan. Dalstroi, to Pavlov

I received the list of those to be rewarded. I regard your list as incomplete; you approached this matter too cautiously and too miserly. In this list you have not included yourself and other members of the top management. Let us reward all, starting with Pavlov, without embarrassment or false modesty. Add another 150-200 persons including several tens of prisoners who have distinguished themselves at work. Remember that the medal "For Labor Valor" is higher than the medal "For Labor Distinction." I don't need any of the details of those to be rewarded. Just send me the names for each type of medal. The list of those freed from prior convictions remains in effect and you can expand it. I am awaiting the general list." Signed, STALIN

Stalin's motivation for this telegram was to raise morale and provide more incentives to a manager operating in a difficult environment. Ten days before his telegram to Pavlov, Stalin reprimanded the local paper *Soviet Kolyma* for criticizing Pavlov's Magadan operation, saying the criticism "does not take into account the difficult conditions of work and the specific conditions of work of Pavlov. Your criticism of Pavlov is unfounded demagoguery. Your newspaper should help Pavlov and not place spokes in the wheel."[5] On the next day, Stalin sent Pavlov a telegram asking him for a list of names of those to be honored.[6]

One can imagine the effect of receiving such a telegram from the supreme and mythical leader, who you thought did not even know of your existence. It also served a practical purpose. It allowed Pavlov to run his mammoth enterprise without newspaper and party officials looking over his shoulder. Stalin's letter of praise was an insurance policy to preserve his job and his life.

Face 2: The Bowing-to-the-Will-of-the-Party Stalin

Except in unguarded moments, there was the fiction that Stalin's orders were never his own but were those of the Central Committee. Stalin's orders were written on Central Committee stationery, sometimes with "J. Stalin" at the bottom but often without a signature.

Among the many victims of Stalin's purge of the party elite was the party boss of Kiev and candidate member of the Politburo, Pavel Postyshev. Postyshev was removed as Kiev party secretary in January of 1937. Stalin reserved Postyshev's fate for the January 1938 Central Committee Plenum, transcripts of which were distributed widely among party members.

The Plenum turned into an unscheduled attack on Postyshev. A series of Stalin cronies condemned him as "bankrupt" and "making crude mistakes for which the party must judge him." Stalin remained silent throughout. At the end, Postyshev was given a chance to repent and begged for mercy:

> I ask the plenum of the Central Committee to forgive me. I never consorted with enemies but I always have battled along with the party against enemies of the people with my whole Bolshevik soul. I made many mistakes, but I did not understand them.

Party members, reading the transcript, would conclude that Stalin was simply carrying out the wishes of others as he summed up the proceeding using the passive tense:

> Here in the Presidium of the Central Committee or in the Politburo, as you wish, the opinion has been formed, that after all that has happened,

it is necessary to take some kind of measures in association with Comrade Postyshev. And it seems as if the following opinion has formed, that it is necessary to remove him as a candidate member of the Politburo, leaving him as a member of the Central Committee.[7]

Postyshev's case was turned over to the party control commission, which recommended his expulsion. Shortly thereafter he was arrested and shot.

Face 3: Stalin the Cynical Flatterer

Stalin could also use the pretext of flattery and charm with extreme cynicism and cruelty on friend and foe alike. On September 25, 1936, Stalin bluntly informed the Politburo that Genrykh Iagoda should be removed as head of the NKVD ("Iagoda is clearly not up to the task . . . "). On the next day, he composed the following memo demoting Iagoda to Minister of Communications:

> Comrade Iagoda:
>   The Ministry of Communications is a very important matter. This is a defense ministry. I do not doubt that you will be able to put it back on its feet. I very much ask you to agree to the work in the Ministry of Communications. Without a good minister we feel as if we are missing our hands. It is not possible to leave the Ministry of Communications in its current situation.[8]

The memo was read [not clear by Stalin or by someone else] from Sochi to Iagoda on the same day at 21:30. Iagoda understood that this memo, which outsiders would interpret as praise, meant the end of his political career and ultimately his life.

It is a puzzle why Stalin engaged in the charade of asking Iagoda "to agree" to the new post and of telling him that without him there it would be like "missing our hands." It could either have satisfied Stalin's enjoyment of mental torture or it could been out of caution. As head of the NKVD, Iagoda had at his disposal special troops and secret agents. Perhaps Stalin thought that flattering words would make Iagoda go quietly.

Iagoda waited six months for his fate to be sealed in a March 31, 1937, Politburo decree:

> In view of the uncovered anti-Soviet and criminal activities of the minister of communication Iagoda, carried out during his work as commissar of the NKVD and also after his transfer to the ministry of communications, the Politburo considers it necessary to exclude him from the party and from the Central Committee and order his immediate arrest.[9]

Iagoda was convicted of espionage and other offenses in March of 1938 and was immediately executed and his body put on display of the grounds of his former dacha.

Face 4: The Unadulterated Stalin

Unlike Hitler's Nazi regime, there was no reluctance on the part of Stalin or his associates to sign death sentences. Stalin's files are full of matter-of-fact approvals of death sentences suggested by subordinates or by his own requests for capital punishments. There are literally hundreds of execution orders signed by Stalin, and they can be broken down into approvals of mass executions, approvals of executions of specific persons, or orders to begin cases or campaigns that will result in executions.

A few examples:[10]

> *Coded telegram to Comrade Andreev in Saratov:*
> The Central Committee agrees with your proposal to bring the former workers of Machine Tractor Station No. 1138 to the courts and execute them.—STALIN, July 28, 1937.

> *Coded telegram to all Party Secretaries:*
> Considering it essential for the political mobilization of collective farmers in favor of destroying enemies in agriculture, the Central Committee requires party organizations to organize in every province and region two to three open show trials of enemies of the people and widely publicize the course of these trials in the local press.—STALIN, August 3, 1937.

To the Smolensk Party Committee:

I advise you to sentence the wreckers of the Andreevskii region to death and publish this in the local press.—STALIN, August 27, 1937.

Extract from the Central Committee minutes:

On the question of the NKVD: To approve the proposal of the Central Committee of Kazakhstan to increase the number of repressed counter-revolutionary elements in Kazakhstan of the first category [automatic death sentence] by 900 and the second category [automatic Gulag sentences] by 3,500, in all 4,400 persons.—SECRETARY OF CENTRAL COMMITTEE [Stalin], December 15, 1937.

To regional Party Secretaries (coded):

In association with the trial of spies and wreckers Tukhachevskii, Uborevich [two respected marshals of the Soviet army], and others, the Central Committee proposes that you organize meetings of workers, and where possible peasants, and also meetings of Red Army units to issue resolutions about the necessity of death sentences. The trial should end this evening. The communication about the sentence [death] will be published tomorrow, that is June 12.—SECRETARY OF CENTRAL COMMITTEE. Stalin, June 11, 1937.

Although these examples relate to the years of the Great Terror, Stalin had been issuing death sentences since the 1920s. For example, in a letter to his deputy Molotov dated August 16, 1929, Stalin ordered "two to three dozen wreckers from the finance ministry and state bank" to be shot, including "common cashiers." In the same letter, he ordered "a whole group of wreckers in the meat industry must definitely be shot."[11]

Although Stalin probably received pleasure from killing his personal rivals, his execution orders were calculated and ordered for a purpose, with Stalin even managing the associated public relations. Village executions taught that the countryside was filled with evil enemies anxious to destroy the achievements of collective agriculture. Increased execution limits signalled that Stalin welcomed more executions in the regions. The public demonstrations demanding the death of Marshals Tukhachevskii and Uborevich were to demonstrate that the death sentences that Stalin had ordered were demanded by the people, and not by Stalin (even though the demonstrations came after the execution sentence). The execution of cashiers was to shift blame for shortages to "evil wreckers" infiltrating the banks.

Dictators and Manners

Stalin gave a first impression of a humble man, a loner, who talked in practical terms, and who lived a simple life. Yet, he could not have attracted to him loyal associates if he lacked social skills. After he achieved absolute power, he could afford to drop his polite approach to his associates, but he could still attract devoted followers. His influence on his ill-fated NKVD head, Nikolai Ezhov, became "total, unlimited, almost hypnotic."[12] Hitler possessed many of the same characteristics. He had excellent manners, lived a simple life, and had the power to charm and attract associates. Like Stalin, he alternated between reasonable discourse and ranting. Hitler truly hated the Jews and "inferior" Slavic races. Stalin truly hated enemies of socialism, which he defined as anyone opposed to him.

Hitler may have resembled Lenin more than Stalin in the fact that he was an armchair executioner. Lenin, while demanding the killing of enemies of Bolshevik power, never pulled the trigger himself. He turned such matters over to fervent subordinates. Lenin was even known as an easy touch for relatives petitioning to commute death sentences. Stalin, on the other hand, personally orchestrated executions and made sure that they went according to his directions. Even when his health did not allow him to actively direct the state and the economy, Stalin continued to read and direct interrogations of political enemies.

What was unique about Stalin and Hitler is that no one anticipated the extent to which they were prepared to carry their brutality. Stalin's decision to liquidate the richer peasants as a class in 1929 brought gasps from the assembled party elite. No one could have known that he would physically annihilate the party elite in the wake of the mysterious assassination of Leningrad party boss Sergei Kirov in December of 1934. Most Germans and many German Jews assumed that Hitler's rhetoric about the Jewish problem was simply words. Stalin took the apparatus of terror created under Lenin, and refined and modified it, but the basic principles of political repression were already in place under Lenin. Stalin's innovation was to apply repression on a scale unimaginable to the first Bolsheviks, which is illustrated in the following Soviet joke, an imagined conversation between Lenin and Stalin:

LENIN: Comrade Stalin, would you sacrifice 10,000 for the Socialist Revolution?

STALIN: Yes, without hesitation.

LENIN: I would as well.

LENIN: Comrade Stalin, would you sacrifice 500,000 for the Socialist Revolution?

STALIN: Yes, without hesitation.

LENIN: I would as well.

LENIN: Comrade Stalin, would you sacrifice ten million for the Socialist Revolution?

STALIN: Yes, without hesitation.

LENIN: You see, Comrade Stalin, in such matters you and I are quite different.

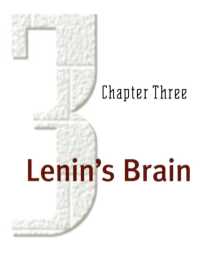

Chapter Three

Lenin's Brain

Background

Vladimir Il'ich Lenin died on January 24, 1924, victim of a fourth and fatal stroke. Since his first stroke in May of 1922, Lenin had struggled with a variety of ailments, including an assassin's bullet lodged near his spine and possibly syphilis. Lenin's death, without an anointed successor, set off a bitter power struggle that ended in December of 1930 with Stalin as the undisputed ruler of Russia.

Stalin's feuds with Lenin had become so inflamed that Lenin, in a political testament dictated from his deathbed, warned that Stalin should be removed as party General Secretary before it was too late. Fortunately for Stalin, Lenin's testament spoke ill of other Bolshevik leaders; there was no rush to make it public even by Stalin's enemies.

We do not know the real origins of the decision, but we do know that a commission of physicians, many of whom had attended Lenin and conducted his autopsy, recommended that his brain be subject to detailed scientific study. Such a study would have suited Stalin's plan to confer sainthood on Lenin. He established, under the auspices of his Central Committee, the Institute of V. I. Lenin shortly after Lenin's demise. Proof that the Lenin Institute was to be a weapon in Stalin's power struggle is found in the naming of Stalin's personal secretary, Ivan Tovstukha, as its managing director. Among Tovstukha's jobs was to gather critical remarks written by Vladimir Il'ich about other party leaders for Stalin's use as compromising material when needed. The "immortalization" of the Great Vladimir Il'ich Lenin was to be accomplished by the display of his embalmed body at the Red Square mausoleum and by the publication of his writings. The Lenin Institute was to provide yet another posthumous honor—scientific proof that Lenin was a genius.

The Institute of Lenin served as a repository for Lenin's writings and for other Lenin memorabilia. Among its most unusual items was Lenin's brain, preserved in a formaldehyde solution in a glass jar. This is the story of the study of Lenin's brain from early 1925 to 1936 as told by the sixty-three–page secret collection of documents from the Central Committee's special files.[1] It is not necessarily a tale about Stalin, although Stalin's guiding hand can be seen throughout. During the early years of these events, decisions about Lenin's brain were likely made collectively by the Politburo, with Stalin always aligned with the majority. After Stalin's assumption of complete power, the matter of Lenin's brain was turned over to his trusted deputy, V. M. Molotov, and Lenin's brain itself was entrusted to a friend from his Georgian youth, A. Enukidze. Throughout the story Stalin was either acutely aware of what was going on or was guiding events.

The file begins three months after Lenin's death, with the decision to study Lenin's brain to prove his genius already made. The story then modulates between Berlin, where a single specimen of Lenin's brain is being studied by a renowned German scientist, Oskar Vogt, and Moscow, where Russian scientists are increasingly lobbying for their own "Institute of the Brain." The Soviets, reluctant to alienate a foreign scientist of international renown, allow Vogt to remain at least nominally in charge of the study, although he is rarely in Moscow where the brain resides. A series of attacks on Vogt's credibility, bearing the markings of Stalin operations, raise questions about his continued role, but it was Hitler's Gestapo that freed Stalin of an independent outside voice. The last entry in the file dates to May 27, 1936, as the nominal head of state, Mikhail Kalinin, distributes to Comrade Stalin and the Politburo "for its examination, the report of the acting director of the Institute of the Brain entitled 'About the study of the brain of V. I. Lenin.'" The Institute of the Brain, indeed, fulfilled its plan. Its report cites indices proving the extraordinary nature of Lenin's brain, while pointing out that the Institute could provide even more convincing evidence if the Politburo awarded it new funds and new premises.

The Story

The story of Lenin's brain begins with a joint proposal to the Politburo from the minister of health, Nikolai Semashko, and Stalin's personal assistant cum deputy director of the Lenin Institute, Ivan Tovstukha, to "export" Lenin's brain to Berlin for study. Semashko and Tovstukha had already received their marching orders: to prove Lenin's genius; they were simply setting up a procedure to deliver the desired results. According to the official account, the proposal to study Lenin's brain originated with a group of eminent scientists and doctors, several of whom had conducted Lenin's autopsy.

Despite their political savvy, Semashko (who initiated the first purge of non-Soviet doctors for Lenin) and Tovstukha (who conducted dirty tricks for Stalin) begin with an error that would jeopardize the politics of the study for the next decade: They proposed to turn the study of Lenin's brain over to Professor Oskar Vogt of the Neurobiological Institute of the Kaiser Wilhelm Institute of Berlin, as the "only world specialist on this question." Lenin's brain should be transferred to Vogt's laboratories in Berlin. Their mistake: Whether Lenin was a genius or dullard would be decided by a foreigner!

Vogt, who had already met with Russian scientists on February 16 and 17, confirmed that it is "possible for such a study to provide a material basis for determining the genius of V. I. Lenin." He proposed to compare Lenin's brain with other brains, an undertaking that required enormous experience, care, and facilities. Vogt warned against such a study in Moscow and, if measures were not taken immediately, the deteriorating brain could not absorb the dyes required for analysis.

Professor Vogt's warnings must have shaken Semashko and Tovstukha, who could be accused of botching the entire study if Lenin's brain was allowed to deteriorate further. Perhaps they viewed the outsourcing of the project as an easy solution. Yet, as experienced bureaucrats, they must have realized that the Politburo (and Stalin) would not turn Lenin's brain over to a foreigner. Indeed, the Politburo met on February 19 and concluded to "refuse the proposal to export the brain of V. I. Lenin abroad for research and instead to conduct the research in Moscow."

Two days later, Semashko came forward with an alternate proposal. Vogt should take one specimen back to Germany for the purpose of determining whether the brain was losing its value, a more modest proposal which the Politburo approved on the same day (February 21, 1925): "to allow Vogt to export and study one specimen of the brain and, in the case of favorable results, to give him further specimens." (It should be noted that Vogt received only this one specimen throughout the entire history of the study).

Three months later (May 22, 1925), the Politburo approved the Lenin Institute's plan of attack: It approved a contract for Vogt, ordered Semashko and Tovstuhka to find an appropriate building and equipment, and to identify two "communist-physicians" to study under Vogt in Berlin. The head of the secret police, Feliks Dzerzhinskii, was ordered "to identify a reliable comrade to be designated as the responsible depository of Lenin's brain as work on it proceeded." The project design was set: the eminent Vogt was in overall charge; the brain was to remain in Moscow; and "reliable" communist-physicians were to be trained under Vogt. Surely, a communist-physician would know what the party required of him.

The story moves forward more than one year later to January 25, 1926, as the minister of health (Semashko) delivers his progress report to the Politburo. He reports that there are as yet no findings, but a German assistant of Vogt is working on specimens in Moscow in close consultation with Vogt, and two "physician-communists" (Sapir and Sarkisov) have finished a course of study under Vogt in Berlin. The empire-building Semashko points out that, insofar as many brains must be studied for comparative analysis, a scientific institute for the study of the brain in honor of Lenin should be created under his ministry of health. On April 28, 1926, Stalin personally ordered the government to award 154,480 rubles for a Medical Commission for the Study of the Brain of V. I. Lenin within the ministry of health.

Thus, as of mid-1926, a Soviet "Institute of the Brain" had been created with the personal approval of Stalin. At least two "communist-physicians" had been trained in Berlin, but the person in charge of determining Lenin's genius remained an independent German scientist. Although apparently no record was taken, Vogt briefed a "narrow circle" of members of the government at some point in 1927 giving them an account of his preliminary findings and a plan for further research.

For Stalin, having a foreign scientist in control of such a delicate project would not have been acceptable in the long run. Danger lurked in the fact that Vogt, the nominal chairman of the Moscow Brain Institute, edited an international scientific journal that listed his affiliation with both the Moscow and Berlin institutes. Such an arrangement would have been a nightmare for Stalin and Soviet censors—a reputable scientific journal outside the reach of Soviet censorship that could issue a verdict on Lenin's genius or lack thereof with the apparent stamp of approval of the Russian side. Vogt had to be contained without causing an international incident.

We can only speculate about the origins of a January 28, 1928, "report memo" from a Military Commissar, Lamkin, to a Comrade Bubnov of the Political Administration of the Red Army, but it bears the markings of a Stalin operation. Stalin would typically move against opponents after receiving "spontaneous" complaints from below that he himself had orchestrated. Indeed, the dutiful Bubnov passed the memo on to Stalin "for his information."

Lamkin (writing as a mole moving in scientific circles) reports that Vogt's position as director of the Moscow Brain Institute and his editorship of a scientific journal that lists his Moscow affiliation are attracting attention from those who consider it "their party duty" to point out a number of problems. Lamkin (whose own scientific credentials are not given) reports that Vogt's published work "does not satisfy the requirements of our neuropathologists, and does not appear to be sufficiently scientifically grounded." Lamkin further adds: "There are honest discussions about why we do not use for this case our own brain scientists whose erudition is comparable to Vogt's." He then goes on to list them by name, including a Dr. Doinikov, identified as a former assistant of Vogt, who refused the directorship of the Brain Institute on the pretext that he "is working in a different direction," but in fact, he considers the Vogt School "not able to give all that could be done in this field using other experimental sciences." Lamkin's memo ends with a caveat: "It is of course true that such conversations take place in a narrow circle of specialists who are not free of envy of foreign scientists. Therefore it is very difficult to determine the real state of affairs, but it is necessary to do so."

Stalin's strong suit was his extraordinary patience. The Lamkin report was only the first building block in what may have become an orchestrated campaign to deal with the troublesome Vogt. For the time being, Stalin simply filed the Lamkin report. Vogt remained nominal director of the Lenin brain project, protected by his international reputation, but Stalin gradually shifted the Lenin project to his closest associates and political operatives. In January of 1932, four years after the Lamkin report, Stalin's deputy, Molotov, was made the Politburo's project overseer, and Stalin's fellow-Georgian A. Enukidze, the head of Kremlin security, was soon to be placed in charge of Lenin's brain. A. Stetskii, the Head of the Culture and Propaganda Department of the Central Committee, now led the attack on Vogt.

Stetskii's report of April 10, 1932, to "Comrade Stalin" (who carefully underlined its key passages) raised a number of problems: Lenin's brain was being kept under intolerable security conditions. There was no guard and the key was kept by one of the scientific workers. There was currently no work being done on the brain. Professor Vogt had not been in Russia since 1928 and had practically no contact with the institute.

Vogt's worst sin, however, was his public lectures based on the one specimen of Lenin's brain in Berlin. To quote Stetskii: "Vogt's presentations are of a questionable nature; he compares Lenin's brain with those of criminals and assorted other persons. Professor Vogt has a mechanical theory of genius using an anatomic analysis based on the presence of a large number of giant cortical pyramidal cells." Stetskii also complains that Vogt's theory is making a mockery of Vladimir Il'ich's mental acuity because: " In the German encyclopedia of mental illness, a German authority (a Professor Spielmaier) claims that such pyramidal structures are also characteristic of mental retardation. In this connection, a number of evil remarks about Comrade Lenin have been placed in the bourgeois press."

Stetskii ends with two proposals for Stalin: "1) to preserve Lenin's brain in a safe place, maybe in the mausoleum placing responsibility on Enukidze, 2) to cut off the relationship with Professor Vogt, sending two comrades to Berlin to take back the specimen of Lenin's brain."

The Politburo met three days after Stetskii's indictment of Vogt, and its actions were, at first glance, puzzling. The Politburo agreed to establish an independent Brain Institute, now subordinated to the Scientific Committee of the Central Executive Committee. Vogt was to be invited to be its director, and "communist-physician" Sarkisov was named as deputy director. The fourth point reads: "to send Comrade Sarkisov to Berlin for two weeks for negotiations with Professor Vogt." On the surface, these negotiations were to persuade Vogt to accept the directorship of this new institute; in fact, it may have been a masterful move to finesse Vogt from the project, while blaming Hitler.

What happened in Berlin in 1932 is described four years later in a February 5, 1936, memo from Sarkisov (now acting director of the Brain Institute) to his boss, Ivan Akulov, of the Central Executive Committee. It turns out that, prior to Sarkisov's visit, the Soviet ambassador to Germany had reported that Vogt had fallen out of favor with Hitler. In the course of Sarkisov's meetings, Vogt confirmed that his apartment had been searched and his telephone conversations bugged. Sarkisov (writing later in his 1936 memo) reported that, according to the latest news, Vogt had been removed from the directorship of the Kaiser Wilhelm Institute for Brain Research, and his case had been turned over to the interior ministry. (Vogt survived. He was drafted into the army as a private in his sixties as punishment for his transgressions, but he was discharged after six weeks of service).

In other words, Vogt was out, thanks to Hitler. There would be no scandal amongst the international scientific community if Vogt's ties to Moscow were severed. In fact, Vogt graciously acknowledged, according to Sarkisov's account, that the Moscow Brain Institute could carry on its work on Lenin's brain without him, particularly now that he was no longer able to visit Moscow. According to Sarkisov, Vogt was especially impressed with the Moscow Brain Institute's collection of brains of key figures from the sciences and arts, such as Lunacharskii, Bogdanov, Mayakovsky, Tsiolkovskii and other notables. Instead of comparing Lenin's brain with ordinary people, the Moscow scientists could compare him with peers.

In a touch of irony, Vogt requested that the final approval for carrying on without him should come from Tovstukha, who had represented the Soviet government when the initial contract was signed. Upon his return to Moscow, Sarkisov received (obviously without difficulty) Tovstukha's permission to continue the project with a fully Russian team. Sarkisov became "acting director" of the Brain Institute. The Russian team remained on good terms with the eminent Vogt and could use his scientific reputation to support their findings.

Sarkisov's 1936 report noted that the Brain Institute had successfully carried out its work over the past four years without Vogt because: "In the years of its existence, our institute has grown and strengthened such that the absence of Professor Vogt, as its director, did not reflect negatively on our work." Eleven years after the project was started, Sarkisov announced: "I hereby inform you that the Institute is prepared to present to the party and the state the results of its research on the brain of V. I. Lenin."

Akulov went about making preparations for the long-awaited report. In a September 7, 1936, memo to Stalin, Akulov reports that he gave the Brain Institute a month in order to complete its comparative analysis and set a date for the first half of March for the final report. On May 27, 1936, Mikhail Kalinin, Akulov's boss and head of the Central Executive Committee, submitted to Stalin and other members of the Politburo the Brain Institute's ten-page report entitled: "Study of the Brain of V. I. Lenin."

The faded and scarcely legible report is full of scientific jargon that would have confused members of the Politburo, but its message was clear: The Brain Institute had done thorough work (153 pages and fifteen albums, and 30,953 brain slices). Lenin's brain had been compared with the brains of ten "average people" and with the brains of leading figures, such as Skvortsov-Stepanov, Mayakovsky, Bogdanov, and even Nobel Laureate I. V. Pavlov, who had died in February of 1936 and could be added to the brain collection. Excerpts from the report speak about an exceptional "high organization" of the brain and other indices "which are associated with an especially high functioning of Lenin's brain in the areas of speech, recognition, and action" and "with processes requiring great diversity and richness of cognitive powers, in other words, with an exceptionally high functioning of the higher nervous system." Lenin's brain "possessed such a high degree of organization that during the time of his illness, regardless of the great damage, it functioned at a high level." Their comparative analysis with the brains of prominent persons showed that Lenin had large pyramidal cells in the third layer of the cerebral cortex—Vogt's

Sketch of Lenin showing his prominent forehead, presumably a sign of genius.

initial finding and his "proof" of Lenin's genius—and that Lenin's brain had ratios of the temporal lobe to the total brain mass superior to those of the poet Mayakovsky and physician-philosopher-science fiction writer Bogdanov.

Sarkisov's presentation ends with self praise and a plea for funds: "From humble beginnings as a small laboratory, the institute has grown into a large scientific-research establishment possessing capabilities to carry out research in the most complex new spheres of neurological science recognized by our own scientists and by scientists of the West."

The reward for such good work: a decree of the Politburo to create a commission comprised of those making the report to study the work of the assessment of Lenin's brain. The final point is an order to the Central Executive Committee to organize a special facility in the institute with specialized equipment for the preservation of the brains of leading personalities.

Lessons

The story of Lenin's brain continues to fascinate. It has been the subject of a novel,[2] and scientific papers about Vogt and his work on Lenin's brain continue to be published in scientific journals to the present day. As told above, the story extracted from the official Soviet archives raises a number of questions and puzzles.

The first of these is why Stalin appeared to be paving the way for Vogt's removal from the project. Vogt, in his public lectures and writings, represented the view that Lenin's brain showed distinct anatomic signs of genius. Apparently, this is what he told a "small group of Soviet leaders" in 1929. Why then did he represent a danger to the Soviet side? Vogt operated in the area of international science, where debate and counter-hypotheses are welcomed, not in the controlled environment of Soviet science. Vogt's findings of Lenin's genius could be publicly challenged and even turned on their head, such as the counter-argument that Lenin's "giant pyramidal cells" could also be indicators of mental retardation. In "Soviet" science there were no counter-arguments, especially when it was the party line that Lenin was a genius.

The second puzzle is why the Central Committee's files on Lenin's brain were included by Russian archivists in the archival collection (Fond 89) "The Communist Party on Trial." This archival collection was created as evidence for prosecutors in the trial of the Communist Party, which took place early in the Yeltsin regime (and never addressed the key issue of past terror). The inclusion of these files, therefore, meant that they somehow provide evidence of misdeeds or crimes. But what was the crime or misdeed in this case?

The "crime" that the Lenin brain file discloses was the extreme elitism of the Soviet regime. Although the Soviet Union was a "worker-peasant state," workers and peasants were not to be in charge; the state was to be run on their behalf by a Stalin or a Politburo. Workers and peasants were to be controlled by wise and even genial Bolsheviks who knew what was good for the masses. In their own conversations, the Bolsheviks spoke of peasants and workers with derision. In a Politburo meeting of the mid-1920s, peasants were described as so greedy they would grab a small bit of land even if it belonged to Saint Peter. Workers were sullen, unwilling to work, and unreliable. Lenin, until the Bolshevik revolution, had never met a worker or been in a factory. Without this enlightened elite to manage these unruly masses, there would never be a peasant-worker paradise.

By this logic, the creators of this dictatorship of the proletariat must themselves be head and shoulders above the rest. This thought was expressed by Leon Trotsky reporting on Lenin's worsening physical condition: "Lenin was a genius, a genius is born once in a century, and the history of the world knows only two geniuses as leaders of the working class: Marx and Lenin. No genius can be created even by the decree of the strongest and most disciplined party, but the party can try as far as it is possible to make up for the genius as long as he is missing, by doubling its collective exertions." [3]

Vogt's comparison of Lenin's brain with those of "ordinary people" and even criminals would therefore be the ultimate sacrilege. More politically correct Soviet scientists approached this sensitive topic with much greater delicacy by comparing Lenin's brain with those of leading figures of the sciences and arts, but even here they had to obtain Trotsky's result—to demonstrate that Lenin's brain was superior even to prominent scientists and literary figures.

The final puzzle is why, after waiting eleven years for the result, Stalin failed to publicize Lenin's genius through the controlled Soviet press? One explanation may have been that by 1936, at the very time when Stalin was executing his most prominent political rivals, he did not want to remind the party of a "genius" Lenin, who might have treated his enemies more humanely. It may also be that the habit of secrecy was too hard to break. All the documents in the file from 1925 to 1936 are labeled "secret" or "top secret." At no point was there an announcement that Lenin's brain was being studied. To inform the public that Soviet scientists had found that Lenin was a genius was more than the security conscious Soviet leadership was prepared to bear.

Chapter Four

Marginals and Former People

Background

The Bolsheviks promised to build a worker's paradise in which a modern industry would produce goods in such abundance that everyone's needs could be satisfied. It would be a privilege and a pleasure for those fortunate enough to live in this worker's El Dorado. But who were these "people" for whom the worker's paradise was being built, with great sacrifice? Who was not to be invited?

According to Bolshevik logic, people were simply the labor needed to build socialism. The use of terms by an alleged proponent of a more humane form of socialism, Nikolai Bukharin, is telling. According to him, the task of the socialist revolution is "to create *communist human material* [author's italics] from *capitalist human material*."[1] In a socialist state with scientific planning, people are not individuals but "material" in the production process. Bukharin's policy prescription was to use "proletarian force ranging from execution to punishment of labor violations" to ensure the proper transformation into communist human material. Those who did not contribute to the building of socialism should not enjoy its benefits.

The Bolsheviks singled out "marginals" and "former people" as those who were not properly transitioning from capitalist to communist human material. This chapter is about these outcasts of Soviet society and how Stalin's Russia dealt with them.

Marginals and Former People: Definitions

In Stalin's Russia, a "marginal" was someone who was not contributing to the building of socialism. Marginals could be slackers, unemployed persons, alcoholics, vandals, petty criminals, rowdies, or even persons without a roof over their heads. In other times and places, most of them would be regarded, probably with sympathy, as the unfortunates of society.

The Bolsheviks viewed marginals as not contributing to society, and, as such, deserving not of society's benefits but of punishment. The concept of "marginals" was broad and included those who came to work late, or not at all, changed jobs without permission, or worse did not hold down a job. They would not show up as volunteers to gather harvests, and they may have been heard to make uncomplimentary comments about the Soviet leadership. The disease of "marginalism," moreover, could spread. In a remarkable lack of faith in the appeal of socialism, Bolshevik leaders believed the adage that "one rotten apple could spoil the bunch." One marginal in a factory might lure honest

Painting by Vladimirov of a former person.

communist "material" to drink, become lazy, or say bad things about Stalin. They would have to be dealt with eventually.

The language of Bolshevism also refers to "former people" (*byv-shie liudi*), who, through their offenses against the state, should no longer be regarded as human beings. Among the ranks of "former people" were supporters of the old regime, religious persons, merchants, land owners, members of banned political parties, richer peasants, professors, teachers, and persons who had traveled abroad or who had relatives abroad. The categories of former people were infinitely flexible. When the head of the Leningrad NKVD in 1935 proposed cleansing Leningrad of "former people,"[2] his list included an eclectic mixture: those who "escaped punishment, not leaving the boundaries of Leningrad and living in their former apartments, those who have relations with relatives and acquaintances living abroad, those who organize discussions criticizing Soviet power, those not carrying out any useful activity but living in Leningrad only because they have a passport, and family members of executed spies, diversionists and terrorists, who, as indirect accomplices, escaped punishment."

Punishing Marginals and Former People

Dealing with marginals was far from the minds of the new Bolshevik rulers in 1917. Their immediate concern were the most dangerous former people such as White Guards, Mensheviks, Social Revolutionaries, and intellectuals. By the mid-1930s, they had been dealt with; attention could turn to marginals and former people.[3]

It mattered a great deal to Stalin where his enemies were located. Only some fifteen percent of the population lived in cities and it was important to have the right "human material" to work in industry. The Bolsheviks' own experience showed that control of one city, Petrograd, brought them to power in 1917. Peasants resisting Soviet power in the countryside were less dangerous if located outside the area of "continuous collectivization." The most dangerous peasants were executed, imprisoned, or deported during the dekulakization campaign of 1930–1932. Their removal brought the heartland of agriculture under the control of Soviet power.

The cities were another matter. There were alarming signs that the cities were being overrun by undesirable elements. Following the deportations in the early 1930s, peasants fled to cities along with other undesirables such as religious officials and supporters of the old regime. In less than a decade, the Soviet Union became an urbanized society as people fled the countryside, where work was hard and unrewarding and life was dangerous for anyone harboring anti-Soviet ideas. Moreover, the cities were already full of marginals who were slowing down production and infecting honest workers with their bad habits.

It was the head of the police and deputy head of the OGPU (the predecessor to the NKVD), Genrykh Iagoda, who was charged with the campaign to clear the cities of such undesirables. Under Iagoda's direction, the police had routinely rounded up marginals, maintained card catalogs on them, and kept them under surveillance. After some debate within police circles, it was decided that prostitutes be also kept under surveillance (despite the fact that there were so many of them) because they were valuable informants.

Faced with burgeoning cities, teeming with undesirables, a state decree of December 27, 1932, ordered the OGPU to introduce a "passport system." Henceforth, citizens had to be registered and be issued passports to live in the most important metropolitan and industrial centers. Those not having the right to passports were to leave voluntarily and quickly. If they did not, they were to be arrested for violating the passport regime.

On January 5, 1933, Iagoda's OGPU issued Decree No. 009 "About Chekist measures for introducing the passport system." As the first step toward cleansing the cities. Iagoda ordered the preparation of lists of anti-Soviet elements for removal from the cities. The announcement of passportization caused some 400,000 to flee the cities in the first half of 1933 alone. They did not wish their pasts to be examined by the OGPU or police. Many had purchased forged papers that would not withstand careful scrutiny. Others remained behind, hoping to blend in. By August of 1934, twenty-seven million passports had been issued in the Russian republic alone. Three to eleven percent of applicants were denied passports; most undesirables probably did not even bother to apply.[4]

Undesirables and Their Punishment

Iagoda's OGPU circular No. 96 "About the procedure for the extra-judicial repression of citizens violating the passport law of August 13, 1933" set the rules for cleansing regime cities. As an extraordinary decree, Iagoda's passportization decree set aside normal court proceedings. Instead, violators were to be punished by special OGPU troikas (called passport troikas) that were manned by OGPU representatives with "oversight" from the prosecutor's office. The troikas were instructed to turn over cases in forty-eight hours to avoid congestion. In addition to their regular registration activities, the OGPU and militia raided housing complexes and made organized sweeps of railway stations and open-air markets to capture unregistered persons and those already denied passports.

Iagoda's decree clearly spelled out the punishment to be meted out by the troika:[5]

The troikas should select measures of extra-judicial repression according to the following examples, allowing for certain variation according to circumstances.

Category of Persons	Measures of Repression
Non-working persons, drifters, and disorganizers of production.	Prohibition to live in the regime city. In the case of a repeated offense— up to three years in a labor colony.
Those deprived of right to vote, kulaks, and de-kulakized persons.	To be sent to labor colonies for up to three years.
Those serving out temporary imprisonment or banishment.	To be sent to special settlements up to three years; in the case of forcible arrest—up to three years in camps.
Criminals and other anti-Soviet elements.	To be sent to camps up to three years.

Those sentenced for violations of the passport regime were sent either to labor colonies, from which they could not leave, or to the Gulag's "corrective-labor camps" where they were incarcerated. Given the intense need for Gulag labor at the time, many ended up in corrective labor camps irrespective of the sentence.

Passport laws remained in force until the end of the Soviet Union to protect cities from "hostile anti-Soviet elements." The right to live in "regime" cities was granted by the state as a privilege. Residence in a regime city meant better rations and better jobs; those in other locations lived a drab and dreary life at a lower standard of living and with fewer opportunities. Those excluded could only dream of living in a Moscow, Leningrad, or a Kiev. Yet the lure of cities was strong, and people continued to violate passport laws. Between 1937 and 1955, 435,000 were sentenced for violating passport laws.[6]

The final reckoning with marginals and former persons came with the Great Terror in 1937–1938, which either executed or imprisoned in Gulag camps more than a half million persons classified as marginals or former people. In fact, the catalogs of hostile Soviet elements compiled for the passport campaign proved invaluable for the selection of victims of the Great Terror.

The Terminology of Desensitization

The Bolsheviks and Stalin did not use terms like "marginals" or "former persons" idly; the terms were used to convince the population at large that such persons were deserving of punishment and were, in a way, inhuman or non-humans. The Soviet system was grounded on the principle of repression, and it was vital that the population not have sympathy with its victims. The NKVD officers charged with executing hundreds of thousands of victims between 1937–1938, most of whom appeared quite normal, were taught to speak of their victims as "troika material." A dedicated NKVD executioner declared in 1937 that it would be a shame if he could not process all his arrestees for execution because "we are dealing here exclusively with riffraff."[7] The term "former people" also implies someone who is no longer a person, and, as such, is not deserving of pity. Gulag guards were subjected to a drumbeat of propaganda that inmates were saboteurs, spies, assassins, the worst types of criminals, and posed an imminent danger not only to society but also to the guards.

The following document, written by the second-in-command of

the Gulag, makes the point that the cities were fortunate to be rid of this rabble:

> Those déclassé elements sent from Moscow and Leningrad to the work colonies of the OGPU are primarily evil recidivists who have a number of offenses and convictions. Our experience at transport points and new settlements shows that they cannot adapt to the routine of the free labor regime of worker settlements. They do not cooperate and they demoralize others. According to the OGPU representative in Western Siberia [a Comrade Alekseev], there were a series of escape attempts, attacks on convoys, and thefts of ration materials. They prey on weaker persons.[8]

The ending of the memo, however, casts doubt on its true intent. The Gulag official, it appears, is simply reinforcing a decision made higher up to re-sentence "evil recidivists" to the Gulag camps, where labor is in short supply:

> In connection with these facts and considering your decree to send this contingent to the camps, I request your directive about the transfer of their cases to OGPU troikas to process them for camps.

Were they being transferred to the camps because they were truly regarded as evil, or because their labor was needed? We cannot answer this question from the material we have at hand; it remains one of the major research issues surrounding the Gulag.

Chapter Five

The Great Terror

Directive No. 00447

The first category includes the most dangerous and most hostile of the above listed elements. They [75,900 of them] should be immediately arrested and after examination of their cases by troikas—BE SHOT.

—*Nikolai Ezhov, Head of the NKVD, July 30, 1937*

The Chief of the Security Police and the SD then gave a short report of the struggle which has been carried on thus far against this enemy, the essential points being the following: a) the expulsion of the Jews from every sphere of life of the German people, b) the expulsion of the Jews from the living space of the German people.

—*Protocol of the Wannsee Conference on the Final Solution, Berlin, January 20, 1942*[1]

Background

The tragic decade, 1935 to 1945, saw two mass slaughters ordered by heads of state—Stalin's Great Terror and Hitler's "final solution of the Jewish problem." State-sponsored terror campaigns such as these cannot be improvised. They need careful preparation. Victims must be identified according to some system; they must be arrested and transported; and they must be executed or imprisoned. Records must be kept on them. The "plan" for Hitler's final solution was put in place on January 20, 1942, at a villa-held meeting in Berlin's Wannsee district, attended by mid-level functionaries. The plan for Stalin's Great Terror was outlined by Stalin himself and was announced on July 30, 1937, by NKVD chief Nikolai Ezhov's Operational Decree No. 00447 "About operations for the repression of former kulaks, criminals, and other anti-Soviet elements." Eighteen months later, 681,000 persons had been shot under this decree.

Ezhov shared the same fate as his victims. Needing a scapegoat for the excesses of the Great Terror, Stalin fired him in November of 1938. Ezhov was executed the night of February 2, 1940. According to an official witness: "He started to hiccup, weep, and when he was conveyed to 'the place,' they had to drag him by the hands along the floor. He struggled and screamed terribly." [2]

This chapter tells the story of Operational Order No. 00447's prehistory, implementation, and consequences.[3] It is largely told in the words of the order itself. Ezhov's July 30, 1937, decree qualifies as the most brutal state decree of the twentieth century. It is remarkable in that it clearly and without euphemisms (such as the Nazi use of "emigration" in place of "extermination") spells out the logic and procedures of Stalin's mass repressions with absolutely no effort to hide its intentions. As its title implies, it was an operational order—a cookbook used by thousands of NKVD officials and party activists to carry terror to the remote corners of the vast Soviet Union.

The Great Terror

Stalin's Great Terror[4] is often confused with his purge of the party elite, which began on the day of Leningrad boss Sergei Kirov's assassination: December 1, 1934. Of the 1,966 elite party delegates to the Seventeenth Party Congress of 1934, 1,108 were arrested on charges of anti-revolutionary crimes and 848 were executed in the course of these purges. The decimated party elite was replaced by a new generation of leaders. But party losses, even of these magnitudes, account for only a small fraction of one percent of total repressions between 1937 and 1938. The average victim was a regular person, holding a normal job and leading an average life.

It was not until the end of July 1937 that Stalin was ready for the "mass operations" stage of his Great Terror. In September of 1936, he replaced the soon-to-be-executed Genrykh Iagoda with the fanatical

Photograph of Nikolai Ezhov on top of the Lenin Mausoleum, May 1, 1938.

Nikolai Ezhov as head of the NKVD. Over the next year, Stalin and Ezhov prepared the "once and for all time" elimination of enemies of Soviet power.

Despite earlier mass campaigns, Stalin remained convinced that his enemies were multiplying. Members of banned political parties had been removed from responsible offices, but they were still alive. German, Lithuanian, and Polish workers were still employed in defense factories. Two million citizens had been "disenfranchised" as politically unreliable.[5] The victims of the 1930–1932 collectivization and dekulakization campaigns were finishing their prison or exile terms, and as many as a quarter million kulaks had fled to the cities or illegally blended into collective farms.[6] Regional party secretaries and NKVD officials warned Stalin of "growing bases for insurgent rebellions" and of large influxes of "alien elements" into their territories. Outlandish tales of mass poisonings and sinister plots spread, encouraged by the fantastic confessions of former party leaders at the Moscow Show Trials. An alarmed Stalin called for increased vigilance to "check every party member and every non-party Bolshevik."[7]

Ezhov's Order No. 00447 was designed to solve a major logistic and operational task: the elimination, through execution or long prison sentences, of a large number of persons whom Stalin considered to be his enemies in a short period of time. In its original form, Order No. 00447 called for the execution of 75,950 and the imprisonment of 193,000 in four months' time, from start to finish. With a five-day week, this target required 883 executions and 2240 prison sentences per day. Victims had to be identified quickly, evidence had to be kept to a minimum, and the pace of operations could not be slowed down by judicial proceedings. Even with its limited protection of civil rights, the "regular" justice system could not produce such numbers. Rather, extraordinary measures had to set aside existing rules and "justice" had to be dispensed with "simplified procedures." Ezhov's decree constructed a "conveyer" (the term used in 1937–1938 to describe the Great Terror) to process large numbers of victims.

Starting the Great Terror

Stalin set "mass operations" in motion with a top secret telegram of July 3, 1937, which ordered sixty-five regions, within five days, to prepare lists of enemies "to be shot" and to staff extra-judicial tribunals (called troikas) for expeditious sentencing.[8] Orders from Stalin or the Politburo were top secret; they could not be shared with others. It was up to the executing agency, in this case Ezhov's NKVD, to issue detailed instructions to those on the ground. Ezhov's Operational Decree of the NKVD No. 00447, issued on July 30, 1937, told the executors what was expected of them.

Mass operations of such magnitude, conducted in sixty-five regions in the world's largest country according to land mass, had to be explained in clear and exacting terms. Each of the sixty-five administrative regions had to know when to start, how many to execute or imprison, how to prepare the paperwork, and who was to carry out the sentence.

Stalin's July 3, 1937, directive gave only the basic outline: Enemies were to be divided into two categories: one to be executed, the other to be sent to remote areas; enemies were labeled with the catch-all phrase "returning kulaks [the term used to describe more prosperous peasants] and criminals." In the almost four weeks between Stalin's telegram and Directive 00447, Ezhov held conferences in Moscow with regional NKVD leaders and met fifteen times with Stalin (often with the indispensable Molotov in attendance) in meetings sometimes lasting more than three hours.

Ezhov had only an elementary education; his drafting skills were weak. The decree was written by his deputy M. P. Frinovskii, whom Ezhov placed in charge of overall operations. Stalin knew and approved its contents. Upon receipt of the Frinovskii draft, Stalin instructed his personal secretary: "I am sending you Operational Decree No. 00447. I request you send this to members of the Politburo for voting and send the results to Comrade Ezhov."[9] The result of the vote was preordained; no Politburo member would dare oppose Stalin on such an issue.

Initially, the regions were told they had five days to prepare lists of victims; so their activity was frantic. Ezhov's NKVD had extensive card catalogs of citizens (internal passport records, criminal records, those expelled from the party, and records of disenfranchised persons) from which centralized lists could be compiled. The regional party and NKVD departments also had extensive regional records from local surveillance, factory lists, and local prosecutors. Moscow, Leningrad, and Kiev officials even kept lists of relatives of those expelled from the party and of former oppositionists.

The decree itself was a classic Soviet "extraordinary decree" that set aside existing legal codes for a designated period of time—a sort of declaration of martial law—and put in place new rules that were to guide the terror campaign from start to finish.

Ezhov's Operational Decree No. 00447 is a document that can largely tell its own story in its own words.

Statement of Purpose

Operational Decree No. 00447 begins by emphasizing the acute danger posed by the enemies of Soviet power. Enemies are described as those who were repressed in earlier campaigns, such as kulaks, sup-porters of the old regime, sectarians, former officials, or those who escaped repression by hiding in villages and by working in strategic factories and construction sites. This time there was to be no dilly-dallying. The most merciless measures were to be used to put an end "once and for all time" to the "foul subversive work" of the masses of enemies at large in Soviet society. In the language of 00447:

> Formations of substantial numbers of former kulaks, earlier repressed persons, those concealing themselves from repression, escapees from camps, work colonies, or deportation have been detected by investiga-tions of anti-Soviet groupings. There are many formations of formerly repressed religious persons and sectarians, and former active partici-pants in anti-Soviet armed activities. They have remained almost un-touched in the village. They include large cadres of anti-Soviet political parties (listed), and also cadres of former activists in bandit rebellions, members of White punitive organizations, repatriates, and so on. Some, leaving the village for the city, have infiltrated industrial enterprises, transport, and construction. Moreover, significant numbers of criminals, thieves-recidivists, pillagers and others serving out sentences, escaping from places of confinement, and hiding from repression are accumulat-ing in villages and cities. The inadequate battle against these criminal contingents has created conditions that support their criminal activities. The organs of state security are faced with the task—in the most mer-ciless fashion—to destroy this band of anti-Soviet elements, to protect the working Soviet population from their counter-revolutionary intrigues and, finally, once and for all, to put an end to their foul subversive work against the foundations of the Soviet state.[10]

Schedule

As an extraordinary decree, Order 00447 set aside existing criminal laws for the period of the campaign. Given the size of the Soviet Union and transport difficulties, the campaign could not start every-where at once. Ezhov set the starting date for August 5 for the cen-tral regions and an ending point four months later. Also, instruction had to be given on which enemies to attack first; namely, the most dangerous "first category." A notable feature of the Order is Ezhov's use of the first person, establishing his personal role and instructing NKVD subordinates to contact him directly for orders. In the language of 00447:

> In connection with this, I ORDER: to begin in all republics, regions and provinces operations for the repression of former kulaks, active anti-Soviet elements and criminals on August 5, 1937. Operations will begin in Uzbek, Turkmen, Tadzhik and Kirgiz republics on August 10, and in the Far Eastern and Krasnoyarsk regions and in Eastern Siberia on August 15. Operations should end within a four-month period.[11]
>
> Contingents of the second category are not to be repressed until special instructions are issued. In cases where a commissar of the republican NKVD, or a head of an administration or of a provincial department, having completed first-category operations, considers it possible to begin operations on the second category, he is required to ask my permission and only after that to start the operation.[12]

Contingents of Enemies

Order No. 00447 lists nine categories of "contingents" of enemies. Although the list appears to focus on kulaks and criminals, Ezhov's definition of enemies includes virtually anyone associated with the former regime, belonging to a political party other than the Bolshevik party, active in a church or religion, returning from abroad, or engaging in "diversionist" activity (whatever that might mean). Striking, also, is the fact that having served out a sentence did not provide an exemption. The most hated contingent, "former kulaks," were to be repressed even after "serving out their term of punishment." Although enemies are characterized in many cases as "conducting anti-Soviet activity," implicit is the fact that individuals are enemies for being who they are not for what they do. No matter how sincere their current support for the Bolshevik regime, former White Guard officers, priests, or Mensheviks remain "enemies of the Soviet state." They are "socially dangerous" without actually doing anything against the state. Whereas earlier certain groups were left untouched, such as members of collective farms, now anyone in any location or employment can be an enemy of the state. In the language of 00447:

I. Contingents (Quotas) Subject to Repression

1. Former kulaks, returning after serving out their punishment and continuing to conduct active anti-Soviet subversive activity.
2. Former kulaks escaping from camps or labor colonies carrying out anti-Soviet activity.
3. Former kulaks and socially dangerous elements, belonging to rebellious, fascist, terrorist, and bandit formations, serving out their terms, hiding from repression or escaping from places of confinement and resuming their anti-Soviet criminal activity.
4. Members of anti-soviet parties (listed), former Whites, gendarmes, officials, members of punitive organizations, bandits, and gang members, accomplices, those assisting escapes, re-emigrants, those hiding from repression, fleeing from places of confinement and continuing to conduct anti-Soviet activity.
5. Those exposed as a result of investigations as the most hostile and active participants in currently-being-liquidated Cossack-White Guard insurgent organizations, fascist, terrorist, espionage-diversionist counter-revolutionary formations.
6. The most active anti-Soviet elements among former kulaks, members of punitive bodies, bandits, sectarian activists, church officials and others currently being held in prisons, camps, work colonies and continuing to carry out active anti-Soviet insurgency work.
7. Criminals (bandits, thieves, recidivist thieves, professional contrabandists, swindler-recidivists, livestock thieves) carrying out criminal activity and circulating in criminal milieu.
8. Criminal elements located in camps and work colonies and conducting criminal activity.
9. All the above elements currently located in villages—in collective farms, state farms, agricultural enterprises and in cities—in industrial and trade enterprises, transport, in Soviet institutions and in construction are subject to repression.[13]

Limits and Requests for Higher Limits

Order 00447 was a Soviet-style plan; only its product was not steel or trucks, but executions and prison terms. A plan is not a plan without plan targets, and, insofar as enemies of the Soviet state are distributed geographically, Operational Decree No. 00447 assigned execution and imprisonment targets—called "limits"—on a regional basis. Each of the sixty-five regions was assigned "limits" for the number of first category, or "most dangerous and hostile," offenders to "be shot" and for a second category to be sentenced to eight- to ten-year terms in camps. The Gulag camps were grouped together as a sixty-fifth region; its inmates were automatically placed in the first category; they were already in prison. The sixty-five regional limits (which we do not reproduce due to space limitation) ranged from lows of four hundred for small areas like Komi or the Kalmyk province to a high of 35,000 for Moscow province. The largest numbers of executions were scheduled for the Gulag (10,000) and for Moscow and Leningrad province and Western Siberia (4,000 each). The totals are not given but they add up to 75,950 executions and 193,000 prison sentences.

In economic planning, plant managers rarely asked for higher plans; Ezhov's terror plan, however, encouraged requests for higher limits: "In cases where circumstances demand a raising of limits," regional NKVD offices "must present to me [again the use of first person] petitions justifying the request." This hint from Ezhov was taken to heart by the sixty-five regions, whose leaders concluded that to not ask for higher limits would be taken as a sign of "bureaucratic inertia" or even taken as the action of a class enemy. Requests for higher limits flooded into Ezhov's and Stalin's offices in a frenzy of "socialist competition." In the language of 00447:

II. About Measures of Punishment and the Numbers of Those To Be Repressed

1. All kulaks, criminals and other anti-Soviet elements to be repressed are to be divided into two categories:
   a) The first category includes the most dangerous and most hostile of the above listed elements. They should be immediately arrested and after examination of their cases by troikas are—TO BE SHOT.
   b) In the second category are the remaining less active but nonetheless hostile elements. They are to be arrested and placed in camps for terms of 8 to 10 years, but the most evil and socially dangerous should be sentenced to prisons according to the specification of the troika.

3. The approved figures are for orientation purposes. The heads of the republican NKVDs and the directors of regional and provincial NKVD administrations do not have the authority to exceed them independently. No arbitrary raising of the figures is allowed.[14]

Family Members as Hostages

"Hostages" were allowed from the first days of Bolshevik power. Lenin's Red Terror Decree of September 2, 1918, ordered the secret police (called then the Cheka): "to arrest as hostages prominent representatives of the bourgeoisie: merchants, industrialists, traders, counter-revolutionary priests, and officers who are enemies of Soviet power and confine them in concentration camps."[15] Under the hostage principle, relatives of those committing crimes were held criminally responsible—a principle widely applied to army deserters fleeing across the border.

During Stalin's purges of the party elite, family members were automatically repressed. Wives and children were executed along with their husbands and parents. Promising that family members would be spared was an effective device to extract confessions. (The promises were extended but usually not honored).

Ezhov's directive concerning family members was surprisingly restrained: They were to be spared unless they themselves engaged in anti-Soviet activity or happened to live in major cities or in border areas. In all cases, they were to be "registered and placed under systematic observation."

4. The families of those sentenced according to the first or second category will, as a rule, not be repressed.[16]

Ezhov listed as exceptions family members capable of active anti-Soviet activities, and families of persons repressed in the first category living in border regions or in major metropolitan areas, who should be jailed or deported.

This leniency changed two weeks later with NKVD Decree No. 00486, "About the repression of wives and the placement of children of those convicted of betrayal of the motherland," which ordered the wives of those convicted of counter revolution to the Gulag along with "socially dangerous children" except for pregnant women and wives who turned in their husbands. Underage children were to be sent to NKVD orphanages for upbringing.[17]

Operational Groups and Arrest Procedures

The ground-level executors of the Great Terror were "deputized operational workers" of the NKVD. These seasoned and hardened officers, drawn primarily from the NKVD's State Security Administration, headed the operational groups that arrested and interrogated (and routinely tortured) prisoners, prepared the case files for the troika tribunal, and carried out the sentences. The operational group could not turn the shooting over to others. It was a task they did themselves, often after drinking themselves into a stupor. The operational group was the backbone of the Great Terror, and its head had the power of life or death, as summarized by the declaration of one operational worker: "I am the interrogator, the judge, and the executioner."[18]

According to Russian criminal codes of the time, arrests required permission of the prosecutor's office—a civil agency nominally independent of the NKVD. This protection from arbitrary arrest was a thin reed, given that the prosecutor's office was dictated to by Stalin. As an extraordinary decree, Ezhov's 00447 set aside this minimal protection of civil rights. Ezhov's "order of carrying out operations" gave arrest authority to NKVD officials at the republican, regional, or provincial levels. It was their job to gather "incriminating evidence" for the preparation of arrest lists, which were approved by NKVD superiors. In the language of section three of Order No. 00447:

III. The Order of Carrying Out Operations

3. According to circumstances and local conditions, territories should be divided into operational sectors. An operational group should be formed for each sector, headed by a responsible republican, regional or provincial NKVD official, who is able to organize serious operational tasks. In some cases, the most experienced and talented heads of regional and municipal departments may be named as heads of operational groups.

4. The operational groups must be staffed with the necessary number

of operational workers and should have means of transportation and communication.

In connection with the necessities of the operational situation, military or militia subdivisions may be attached to the group.

5. The director of the operational group should manage interrogations, direct the investigation, confirm the incriminating conclusions, and carry out the sentence of the troika.

6. Detailed data and compromising materials must be gathered for every repressed person. Arrest lists are to be created from such material, signed by the head of the operational group and forwarded in two copies for examination and approval by the NKVD commissar of the republic or the director of the administration of the provincial department of the NKVD, who give permission for the arrest.

7. On the basis of the approved list, the head of the operational group carries out arrests. Every arrest is designed as an order. In the course of the arrest, a careful search is to be conducted. It is necessary to confiscate weapons, ammunition, explosives, poisons, counterrevolutionary literature, precious metals, ingots, foreign currency, duplicating equipment and correspondence. All confiscated material is registered in the search protocol.

8. Those arrested are to be concentrated in points, according to directives of superiors, which should have facilities suited for the accommodation of prisoners.

9. Those arrested will be strictly guarded. All measures should be organized to prevent their escape or other kinds of excesses.[19]

Simplified Procedures and Conspiracies

Operational groups had to fulfill their "limits." If they had too much paperwork or were otherwise restricted, they could not process enemies with sufficient speed. Ezhov's directive, at first glance, appears to impose such administrative burdens. The case file should include the arrest order, search protocol, confiscated materials, and the indictment. Ezhov's allowance of "simplified procedures," a code word to proceed with minimal formalities, however, provided the escape clause for harried operational groups. The work of a head of an operational group in a remote Siberian town (who had arrested one thousand locals) illustrates the flexibility of simplified procedures. Despite complaints that he could only process three cases per day, he somehow managed to submit two hundred and sixty first-category cases in less than two weeks, most of which were approved by the troika.[20] The greatest simplification was the Law of December 1 (passed on the day of Kirov's assassination), which declared that confession was a substitute for objective evidence. Once a confession was extracted, the matter could go directly to the troika. Such simplified procedures allowed the NKVD's "conveyer" of repression to work at full speed.

Order 00447 also instructs that the "investigation should uncover all criminal ties of the arrested party." Isolated enemies of the Soviet regime were not dangerous; they were only dangerous as part of a larger conspiracy. The goal of the interrogation was to incriminate others. Confessions were extracted by appealing to patriotism, promising to spare loved ones, pledging prison instead of death, and, most commonly, torturing. Persons subjected to these techniques implicated friends, fellow workers, and even casual acquaintances. They dutifully confessed to improbable plots, such as Stalin's lifetime friend and fellow Georgian's (A. Enukidze) confession of a plot to assassinate Stalin and other Politburo members,[21] as the transcript of his interrogation shows:

Q: How many persons did you need to carry out the revolt within the Kremlin.
A: Twenty to twenty-five persons.
Q: How many did you have?
A: Fifteen.
Q: Who are they?
   [Enukidze gives their names].
Q: Why didn't you carry it out?
A: We had agreed with Tomsky that I would await his order.
Q: If you had received this order would you have carried it out?
A: Yes.

A low-level official signed a confession of involvement in a conspiracy to assassinate Stalin with people she had never met: "I did not have the strength to resist further. At that time, I did not care if they shot me or sentenced me, and I signed everything that they wanted." Another signed a bizarre confession when promised that life in the camps would be easier than trying to hold out.[22] Ezhov's antiseptic section on investigations conceals their extreme brutality:

IV. Process of Carrying Out Investigations

1. For every arrested party or group of arrested persons, there is to be an investigation. The investigation is to be carried out quickly and in a simplified procedure.

   In the process of the investigation all criminal ties of the arrested should be uncovered.

2. Upon conclusion of the investigation the case should be submitted to the troika for examination.

   In the case material should be included: the arrest order, the search protocol, material confiscated during the search, personal documents, agent-registration material, the protocol of the interrogation, and a short indictment.[23]

Troikas

Another staple of simplified procedures was the troika—an extra-judicial body, comprised of three members, headed by an NKVD official. Troika members were confirmed by the Politburo (Stalin). Once the troika members themselves started being repressed, Stalin had to scramble to keep them staffed. Stalin's correspondence from this period is full of orders to replace Comrade X with Comrade Y in the troika located in region Z.

Troikas date to the first days of Bolshevik power when Lenin used them to dispense summary justice on Bolshevik enemies. Troikas were described by a justice department official (in 1927) as a cosmetic court proceeding to calm foreign critics without compromising the battle against spies and counter-revolutionaries. Troikas were used by the NKVD's predecessor (the OGPU) to sentence kulaks and others opposed to Soviet power to prison or to death in the early 1930s.

Order 00447 required the heads of the operational groups to submit their "cases" to troikas. The troika's job was to confirm the sentence and to order the sentence to be carried out. Troika decisions could not be appealed; troikas were not bound by special procedures, and their sentences were to be carried out immediately. Such a format "ensures the harshness of repression and necessary speed."[24] The cosmetic protection from arbitrary NKVD action offered by the troika was that an NKVD official was only one of three troika members. The other two positions were to be occupied by a prosecutorial official and a party official. In most cases, however, the party and prosecutorial representatives were only extras, and, as the terror proceeded, they themselves were often arrested. One troika met in full form only once,[25] and there were even cases of one-man troikas.

The troika procedures established by Order 00447 gave victims little chance. They were arrested and interrogated by the NKVD operational group, which recommended the sentence (death or prison) to the troika, also headed by an NKVD officer. The troika did not "try" the case; the accused did not appear before the troika and had no defender. The troika's job was to determine that minimal procedures were followed and to confirm the recommended sentence. As the Great Terror progressed, troikas were satisfied with thinner and thinner case files. By 1938, case files listed only the name, address, and profession of the defendant, and gave a one-line indictment ("committed counter-revolutionary acts") and the sentence. Troikas had to process large numbers of cases on a daily basis; there was no time for reviews. The Leningrad troika sentenced 658 defendants to death in a single day (October 9, 1937).[26] The more visible cases went to the military collegium of the Supreme Court of the USSR or of the republics, but the court venue made little difference. Each case and punishment were prepared in advance by the NKVD and approved by the Politburo. Although the accused was present (unlike troikas, which never saw their victims), the typical military collegium case lasted no more than fifteen to twenty minutes, and eighty-five percent concluded with death sentences.[27]

V. ORGANIZATION OF THE WORK OF TROIKAS

1. I confirm the following lists of persons for republican, regional, and provincial troikas [lists of names not included in the document].
2. The republican, regional, or provincial procurator may be present at meetings of the troika (if he is not already a member).
3. The troika will carry out its work or will be located in points where there are corresponding NKVD departments or will go to places where operational sectors are located.

4. Troikas will examine materials for each arrested person or for groups of arrested persons and also for every family subject to exile.

    Troikas may transfer persons arrested as category 1 to category 2 depending upon the character of the material and the degree of social threat and vice versa.

5. Troikas must maintain protocols of their meetings in which are registered the sentence of each person convicted.

    The protocol of the meeting of the troika is to be sent to the head of the operational group for carrying out the sentence. Excerpts from the protocol are to be attached to the investigatory materials for each convicted party.[28]

Carrying out Sentences

The final stage for the victims of the Great Terror was the execution of the sentence approved by the troika. Order 00447 was simple and clear. The troika chairman was to designate the person to carry out the sentence (usually the head of the operational group) and the paperwork was kept to a short excerpt from the meeting of the troika setting the sentence. Executions were to be carried out under conditions of strict secrecy as to time and place. The execution order was to be kept in a separate file, making it more difficult for relatives to learn that their loved one had been executed. Those sentenced to prison were to be dispatched according to instructions from the Gulag administration. Many executions were carried out in killing fields near major urban centers, such as the Butyrskii Poligon near Moscow, but others were carried out in remote locations.

VI. PROCEDURE FOR CARRYING OUT SENTENCES

1. Sentences are carried out by persons according to the directives of the chairman of the troika.

    The materials required for the carrying out of sentences are: certified excerpts from the protocol of the meeting of the troika appended by the sentences for every convicted person and a special order signed by the chairman of the troika to the person assigned to carry out the sentence.

2. Sentences of the first category are to be carried out in places and according to the procedures established by directives of the

commissars of republican NKVDs, heads of administrations and heads of provincial departments of the NKVD with the obligation to maintain full secrecy of the times and places of carrying out the sentence.

Documents concerning the carrying out of the sentence are to be attached in a separate envelope to the investigatory material of every convicted person.

3. The dispatch of persons of the second category to camps is carried out on the basis of assignments from the Gulag administration of the NKVD.

Management of Operations and Records

Ezhov's decree ends with housekeeping matters, such as reporting requirements and the obvious need to prevent escapes. It was clear that Ezhov wished to have an accurate record of executions. It was only later, when relatives clamored for answers, that Ezhov's successors seemed to have difficulty determining the fate of loved ones.

VII. ORGANIZATION OF MANAGEMENT OF OPERATIONS AND RECORDS

1. The general management of operations is placed on the deputy commissar of the NKVD—the head of the main Administration of State Security—Commander Frinovskii.

A special group is to be formed to manage the operation.

2. Protocols of troikas concerning the execution of sentences are to be immediately dispatched to the head of the eighth department of Administration of State Security with the attachment of the inventory card according to form number 1.

For those sentenced to category 1 include with the protocol and inventory card also the investigatory material.

3. Report the course and results of operations in 15-day reports on the 1st, 5th, 10th, 15th, 20th, and 25th days of every month by telegram or in more detail by post.

4. Report immediately by telegraph all newly uncovered counter-revolutionary formations, the appearance of excesses, escapes, the formation of bandit or pillaging groups or other extraordinary events.

Some Thoughts on the Great Terror

The complete openness of written instructions to murder or imprison hundreds of thousands of people, such as Operational Decree No. 00447, tells us that the executioners either believed that what they were doing was right or, if not, that there would be no adverse consequences. Hitler's executioners were more cautious.

Although some fanatics, such as Ezhov and a few of his associates, may have believed the myths of super-human class enemies organizing massive and intricate plots, regular NKVD officials would have known the truth. They knew that confessions were forced by torture or by false promises of leniency. Therefore, the most likely explanation is that most understood that what they were doing was wrong but that they would not be punished, or that they had no choice in the matter anyway.

The absence of caution appears justified. Despite more than a million unwarranted executions and premature deaths, few of those responsible were punished. As Stalin turned off the Great Terror and the search for scapegoats began in November of 1938, only 937 NKVD employees were arrested (91 from the central office), and 99 were reported as deceased, with no information given on the cause of death.[29] They were punished less for their deeds than for their association with discredited superiors who had fallen out of favor with Stalin. They also needed to be liquidated to make room for the new boss's underlings.

As the Gulag began to empty of prisoners after Stalin's death, a number of NKVD officers, interrogators, and informants panicked and a few committed suicide. One interrogator fell to his knees and begged forgiveness. Former inmates, in rare cases, took vengeance into their own hands, such as a former officer who shot his interrogator to death in Kiev. A female informant responsible for the imprisonment of many colleagues was fired from her party job, went insane, and continued to come to work every day to be turned away at the front entrance.[30] In the vast majority of cases, however, those responsible for the imprisonment of millions of persons lived out their lives with no visible repercussions.

Low-level administrators could justify their actions with the claim that they were only following orders—a claim less easily exercised by Politburo members, such as Khrushchev. After addressing an open meeting after he had exposed Stalin's crimes (in 1956), Khrushchev purportedly received a written question asking why he allowed such things to happen. Khrushchev asked the audience who wrote the question and, upon receiving no answer, responded: "He who wrote this question is afraid, just like we were all afraid to act against Stalin." [31]

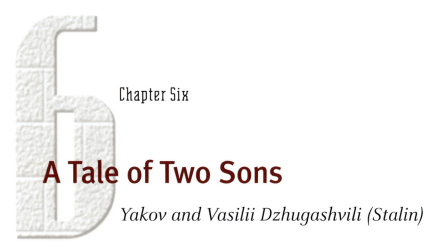

Chapter Six

A Tale of Two Sons

Yakov and Vasilii Dzhugashvili (Stalin)

Background

As in many families, Stalin's two sons were a study in contrast. His first, Yakov, was born in March of 1907 to Stalin's first wife, who died in the same year. His second son, Vasilii, was born in 1921 to his second wife, Nadezhda, who committed suicide when Vasilii was eleven. Both went by the family name of Dzhugashvili.

The elder, Yakov, was introverted, brooding, and sullen. His relationship with his distant and critical father was stormy; a failed suicide attempt prompted only scorn from his father. The younger, Vasilii, and his sister, Svetlana, were raised by nurses and security guards; Vasilii scarcely saw his father. Vasilii was happy-go-lucky, a prankster, a poor student, a bon vivant who enjoyed women, cars, and drinking—the opposite in most respects to his austere father.

During the Second World War, or the Great Patriotic War, as the Russians call it, both sons served in the military, the thirty-four-year-old Yakov as a senior lieutenant and the twenty-year-old Vasilii as a pilot in the Soviet air force. Despite Vasilii's bad grades, he was admitted to a prestigious training school for pilots through the intervention of NKVD head Lavrenty Beriia.

Lieutenant Yakov Dzhugashvili was captured by the Nazis in 1941. Aware that he was Stalin's son, the Nazis offered Yakov in exchange for a German general, a deal Stalin dismissed out of hand as an unfair exchange. Unfortunately for Yakov and for millions of other captured Russians, Stalin believed all captured soldiers were traitors. Yakov disappeared into a German concentration camp, his fate unclear at war's end.

The younger Vasilii's wartime career had a brighter ending. He served as a commander of an LA-7 group and flew 961 missions and took part in fifteen air battles, according to his evaluation of 1945. By the war's end, the twenty-four-year-old Vasilii had risen to the rank of air force colonel and was a recipient of the Medal of the Red Banner. He had before him a promising military career. Although his father took no steps to advance his career, Vasilii's superiors took no chances. Vasilii became accustomed to receiving favorable treatment—a habit that lasted throughout his lifetime.

This is the story of Stalin's two sons as told by their files in the Central Committee archives.[1] Neither story ends well. Yakov's ends with his dead body stretched across the barbed wire of the Sachsenhausen concentration camp. Vasilii's ends with his death from alcoholism in 1962 in a provincial town, after years of prison and disgrace.

Yakov

At war's end, the fate of POW Yakov Dzhugashvili remained unclear, although there were rumors that he had been sent to a concentration camp and had died there. The Nazis would have wanted to keep such a high-profile captive alive, even if his father (Stalin) had refused offers of an exchange. Maybe Stalin would have a change of heart.

Despite Stalin's apparent indifference to his son's fate, the NKVD conducted an investigation from its headquarters in occupied Berlin at war's end. Deputy minister Ivan Serov summarized the results of his investigation into Yakov's fate in a six-page report from Berlin sent on September 14, 1946, to be read "only personally" by his boss, NKVD head Kruglov. There is no information in the files as to whether this report was passed on to Stalin. Kruglov rarely met with Stalin in person; therefore, he would have reported the results to Stalin in writing. Whether he did tell Stalin will remain unknown.

Serov established that Yakov had indeed been transferred to the

Photograph of Yakov Dzhugashvili (Stalin's son) in German captivity.

Sachsenhausen concentration camp. The former chief of guards of Sachsenhausen, a Gustav Wegner, confirmed that there was a special camp for generals and other highly placed Russian officers within the confines of the Sachsenhausen camp. It was in these special barracks that Yakov was held along with a relative of Molotov. Wegner remembered Yakov well and reported a number of conversations with him. Yakov's only request for special treatment was for newspapers, and he never gave his last name. He kept himself apart from other prisoners and appeared in a depressed state. At the end of 1943, Wegner was informed that Yakov had been killed by guards while attempting to escape. Wegner could not (or did not want to) recount the exact circumstances because the investigation was conducted under the lead of Gestapo chief Heinrich Himmler.

The NKVD's interrogation of the camp commander (a Colonel Kainel) also confirmed that Senior Lieutenant Dzugashvili was held three weeks in the camp prison and then, at Himmler's directive, was transferred to the special camp, consisting of three barracks surrounded by a brick wall and high-voltage barbed wire. Kainel reported, consistent with the chief of guards, that Yakov was a solitary figure who shunned contact with other prisoners.

The camp commander reported the circumstances of Yakov's death as follows: The inmates of barrack number 2 were allowed to walk in the early evening in the area outside their barracks. At 7:00 P.M., the SS guards ordered them to return to their barracks. All obeyed except Dzhugashvili, who demanded to see the camp commander. The guard's repeated order went unheeded. As the SS guard telephoned the camp commander, he heard a shot and hung up. Dzhugashvili, in a state of agitation, had run across the neutral zone to the barbed wire. The guard raised his rifle ordering him to stop, but Dzugashvili kept on going. The guard warned that he was going to shoot; Dzhugashvili cursed, grabbed for the barbed-wire gate, and shouted at the guard to shoot. The guard shot him in the head and killed him.

Clearly the unauthorized shooting of none other than Stalin's son set off great apprehension in Sachsenhausen. He had been transferred in by Himmler himself, who hoped to use him as a pawn of some sort. Now, Stalin's son was dead, and no one knew what the consequences would be. Dzhugashvili's body lay stretched across the barbed wire for twenty-four hours while the camp awaited orders from Himmler. The

Gestapo sent two professors to the scene who prepared a document stating that Dzhugashvili was killed by electrocution and that the shot to the head followed. The document stated that the guard acted properly. Dzhugashvili's body was then burned, and the urn with his ashes was sent to the Gestapo headquarters. Indeed, it seemed irrelevant whether Yakov was killed by electrocution or by the bullet. Either way, it was he who committed suicide.

Serov's NKVD interrogators asked for and got an accurate physical description of Dzhugashvili from the camp commander and chief of guards, who also identified him through photographs.

Serov's report ends on a suspicious note that sends a chilling message about NKVD interrogation methods:

> In the course of the investigation it was established that the commandant SS Colonel Kainel and the commander of the guards, SS Lieutenant Colonel Wegner, are not telling everything they know, fearing they will be charged with crimes associated with Sachsenhausen. We have established their intent to commit suicide by attacking the guards or by jumping to their deaths. When we got charge of the former officers of the SS Camp Sahchsenhausen from the Americans, they asked us to turn them over to the court. For this reason, we are not able to apply the full measure of physical intervention [the code word for torture] to Kainel and Wegner. But we did organize to have a mole in their cells.

Vasilii

Vasilii Dzhugashvili (aka Vasilii Stalin) started his active military service in the 16th Aviation Division. His advancement was rapid, from inspector in the air force general staff, to major, and then to colonel. By war's end he was a general. He was then promoted to head the air force's Moscow Military District as a major general. He was demoted by his father from this post in 1952, according to the Central Committee files, for his loose lifestyle and his constant drinking, but he remained in the rank of general.

Although Stalin took no recorded steps to help his son's career, the Stalin name served as a strong shield that evaporated when his father died in March of 1953. Vasilii was arrested on April 29, 1953, one and a half months after his father's death. MVD chief Lavrenty Beriia, who had intervened on Vasilii's behalf before, was arrested by Stalin's successors in June of 1953 and could provide no further assistance.

The MVD was placed in charge of Vasilii's interrogation. The head of the MVD, Kruglov, informed the Politburo on August 8, 1953, that Vasilii Dzhugashvili had confessed to the charges against him, which included:

> Illegal expenditures, theft and diversion for own use of state property and money, forcing subordinates into such illegal acts. In addition, he allowed hostile attacks and engaged in defamatory remarks against the leadership of the party and also expressed his intent to establish ties with foreign correspondents to give interviews about his situation after the death of his father.

Kruglov also reported that Vasilii tried to enlist Beriia's help: "In the course of the past month. V. I. Stalin more than once requested his interrogators to make arrangements for a meeting with Beriia, justifying this request that he wanted to know the Soviet government's decision concerning his fate." Vasilii was obviously isolated or else he would have known that Beriia himself had already been arrested. He probably requested the meeting in the hope that Beriia could bail him out of a difficult situation.

Vasilii's interrogation was conducted from May 9 to 11, 1953, by the notorious head and deputy head of "the investigations division for especially important matters of the ministry of interior." His much-feared interrogators, Vlodzimirskii and Kozlov, were themselves to be arrested shortly as part of Beriia's retinue.

It appears that Vasilii's interrogators did not have to push hard for his confession. He seemed to relish the recounting of his crimes and misdeeds as commander of the Moscow Military District. Most of his crimes relate to high living and expenditure of military funds to support his sports and hunting hobbies. Vasilii's tone is that of a school boy confessing his pranks to the school principal, as the following excerpts show:

> Besides that, my improper conduct expressed itself in systematic drunkenness, sexual encounters with women subordinated to me, and other types of scandalous activities.

In the period from 1947 to 1949, I formed teams of champions in about all types of sports: horseback riding, hockey, motorcycle racing, ice skating, basketball, gymnastics, swimming, and water polo. Besides that I succeeded in gaining the transfer from the air force of its football team. There were more than three hundred athletes in these teams, whose cost was more than five million rubles per year. In connection with organizing the equestrian and motorcycle teams, I ordered three hangars in the central airport to be rebuilt at the expenses of the Moscow military district. One was for the riding hall, the other for horse stables, and the third for motorcycles.

QUESTION: Did you recruit athletes from those serving in the military?

ANSWER: No. There were no military personnel on these teams. They were put together from professional athletes and, according to my command, were taken from other sports teams. . . . In order to attract [a noted athlete by the name of] Starostin, I not only paid him and his wife, but I also arranged a Moscow living permit, which I knew that he, having a criminal record, did not have the right to have. When the militia refused the permit, I ordered my adjutant to settle him in the hunting society of the military district. After a while, Starostin was caught by the militia in his wife's apartment and was told to leave Moscow immediately. Knowing that Starostin had left Moscow, I ordered the former head of counter-intelligence of the military district and his adjutant to commandeer an airplane to overtake his train and bring him to my apartment.

Vasilii's confession proceeds with more tales, which remind one of the exploits of a crooked politician:

In 1950 I named the caretaker of my dacha as deputy coach of the hockey team. Also the teachers of my children were paid by the sports team. I also invited artists from Sochi to do artistic renovations of my dacha and apartment, paying them as hockey coaches of the highest qualification. My personal chauffeurs and even my mistress were paid as swimming coaches although they did nothing of the sort. Persons who worked as my personal servants were paid monthly salaries up to [the princely sum of] two thousand rubles, and they were given apartments in military housing and high quality military clothing destined for pilots and other air force personnel.

QUESTION: Tell us about the hunting society and for what it was created.

ANSWER: The 'hunting society' was created by me in 1948 in a location closed to outsiders on my orders. The 'society' covered a territory of 55,000 hectares. I ordered the construction of three homes and the reconstruction of a narrow-gauge railway, for which a special trolley car was built. I ordered from hunting preserves twenty five-point deer at a cost of 80,000 rubles, and we also got, I don't know from where, beavers and white partridges. Within the Moscow military district, we organized a 'special administration' of the hunting society, the head of which was a reserve captain, who was counted as a coach of the football team. Another nine were listed on various sports teams, including the wife of my dacha caretaker, who was listed as a gymnastics instructor. In actual practice, the entire administration and also the professional hunters and armed guard did nothing because I was there only two times, and no one else was allowed. If an actual hunter had shown up, the guards would have confiscated his weapon and sent him away. I flew to the hunting society in my own airplane accompanied by friends and servants. Another airplane was dispatched to a nearby airport to bring in food, vodka and wine because we were staying several days.

The above excerpts touch only the surface of Vasilii's misuse of state funds, and worse, of military funds for his own use. Other parts of his confession speak to his yachts, foreign automobiles, mistresses, use of foreign exchange, and so on. Clearly, Vasilii Dzhugashvili's interrogators had more than enough to convict him. Although most of his confession related to misuse of state funds, the most serious charges against him were his threats to speak out against the new leadership and to contact the foreign press. It is for this reason that Vasilii Dzhugashvili's eight-year sentence was under the infamous Article 58 of the Russian criminal code for counter-revolutionary offenses.

The sentencing of a personage like Stalin's son required considerable deliberation at the highest levels. Vasilii was sentenced on September 2, 1955, (two years after his arrest) by the Military Collegium of the Supreme Court to eight years of prison on charges of counter-revolutionary activity and theft of state funds.

At this point in the story, Vasilii disappears into a Soviet prison.

Clemency Denied

The Soviet state again addressed Vasilii Dzhugashvili's case on January 5, 1960, after his having served six years and eight months. At that time, prison authorities had reported him as a good prisoner and there was concern about his deteriorating health (heart disease, stomach disorders, and other problems).

Nikita Khrushchev was apparently ready to consider clemency and turned to the head of the KGB and the chief prosecutor for their joint recommendation. The proposed terms were quite generous. Vasilii was to be "granted a partial amnesty, freeing him from the rest of his sentence and the Moscow city government was to be charged to give him a three-room apartment and the ministry of defense was to give him a pension in accordance with the law, along with three months in a sanatorium, to return the personal property taken from him at the time of his arrest, and to give him a one-time payment of 30,000 rubles." The Presidium of the Central Committee appeared ready to accept this proposal and prepared a draft decree on this point on January 8, 1960.

It was probably Vasilii's stubbornness that cost him this generous amnesty. There are no documents on his case between January 8, 1960, and his scheduled release on April 28, 1961. We imagine that Vasilii, when presented with the earlier amnesty proposal, demanded full rehabilitation and restoration to the rank of general—terms the leaders of the Soviet Union could not accept.

The next-to-last memo in the file, dated April 7, 1961, is again from the chief prosecutor and the head of the KGB, written three weeks before Vasilii's scheduled release. The frustrated memo makes clear that Vasilii has been a major irritant. The terms of his release have become more severe. Vasilii has not "corrected himself," acts in a "dark fashion," and "demands special privileges for himself which he had during the life of his father."

Clearly, the Soviet leadership feared that Vasilii would be a loose cannon if allowed to stay in Moscow. Better to bury him in a closed provincial city. When told that he would be sent to Kazan or Kuibyshev, he asserted that he would not voluntarily live anywhere but Moscow. He rejected the proposal to change his name and threatened that if not given appropriate conditions (dacha, apartment, pension, and so forth), "he would not keep quiet, but would tell everyone that he was convicted without foundation and was treated arbitrarily." After his release, Vasilii threatened to meet with N. S. Khrushchev and other members of the Presidium, inform the appropriate offices about his mistreatment, and perhaps ask the Chinese embassy to send him to China, where he could recover his health.

His threat to appeal to the Chinese was not received as an idle one. At the time, the Chinese under Mao were disturbed about Khrushchev's "defamation" of Stalin in his 1956 secret speech. Having Stalin's own son under Chinese wings would have been a powerful propaganda tool in the setting of worsening Sino-Soviet relations. Vasilii's threat to contact foreign journalists also had to be taken seriously. Having a drunken and "dark" son of Stalin spouting off to the international press could have harmed Soviet interests.

What to do with such an ornery person? The verdict: "Because of these actions, we propose to exile him to Kazan (a city where no foreigners are allowed), as an exception to existing legislation. In Kazan, he will be given a single one-room apartment."

The banished Vasilii Dzhugashvili would not be an irritant for long. The KGB reported to Khrushchev on March 9, 1962, that Dzhugashvili (Stalin) Vasilii Iosifovich had died in Kazan earlier that day. "According to preliminary information, the cause of death was alcohol abuse. V. I. Dzhugashvili, despite multiple warnings of his doctor, was systematically drunk. We consider it wise to bury V. I. Dzhugashvili in Kazan without military honors. We request permission to inform his closest relatives. Signed V. Semichastny, Head of the KGB."

Vasilii Dzhugashvili was partially rehabilitated in 1999, when the Military Collegium of the Supreme Court lifted charges of anti-Soviet propaganda that dated from 1953. His body was re-buried in a Moscow cemetery in 2002.

Why No Stalin Dynasty?

The stories of Stalin's two sons are tragic. Both ended badly. Both suffered from Stalin's bullying and neglect. Vasilii became attached to privileges that his father's subordinates showered on him, and his stubborn insistence that he deserved them caused trouble to the very end. Had he been better behaved and more predictable, the post-Stalin leaderships might have looked the other way with respect to his theft of state property. Deep down, Soviet authorities feared the adverse publicity that an unpredictable son of Stalin could bring down on them.

There is another angle to the story of Stalin's sons to consider: Why did their father not groom them to take over after he was gone? In many cases (Duvalier in Haiti and Aliev in Azerbaijan), dictators extend their reign beyond their natural life spans through their sons. Stalin's handling of his sons makes clear that he had no intention of grooming them as successors. Why was this so? We can only speculate, but it seems clear that Stalin made sure that there would be no consideration of successors during his lifetime. He left it to his successors to fight for his position, just as he had fought to succeed Lenin. Whenever rumors circulated that a particular party leader was a likely successor, Stalin brutally cut them down to size. For those who showed independent intiative and ability, Stalin had them killed.

An able and ambitious son of Stalin would have been considered by Stalin as a threat to his power, and Stalin's primary goal was unlimited and unbridled power. It may even have been true that Stalin, through abuse and indifference, made sure that no son of his would ever be considered as a potential successor.

Chapter Seven

Relatives and Falsifying Death Certificates

Background

Ezhov's Operational Decree No. 00447, which initiated the Great Terror, kept sentences separate from case files to make it difficult to trace what happened to the condemned person. Great Terror victims simply disappeared into the NKVD's repression conveyer; especially in cases of capital punishment, their fate was carefully concealed.

Unwitting relatives of those executed were given a standard response: they had been sentenced to ten years in prison "without the right of correspondence." There may have been an underground network that explained the grim meaning of "no correspondence," but probably most clung to the hope that their loved one was alive and toiling away in a Siberian camp.

At the time of Stalin's death in March of 1953, few relatives of the almost three quarters of a million persons executed in 1937 and 1938 had official word on their fate. They, however, could do simple arithmetic. If their loved ones were sentenced to ten years in 1937 or 1938, they should have been released in 1947 or 1948. As this deadline came and went, frustrated petitioners flooded NKVD (now MVD) offices, the justice ministry, and the Politburo with pleas to learn what had happened to their family members.

This chapter tells of the official response to a problem that confronted both the Stalin regime and its successors: how to conceal the fact that three quarters of a million of Soviet citizens were executed in 1937–1938 when it became increasingly obvious that the official story (they are in prison) was not true? The cover-up lasted over sixty years. It was not until after the collapse of the Soviet Union that re-pressed persons and their survivors received the official right to view their case files.

The Cover-up

By 1951, the Ministry of State Security, now independent of the in-terior ministry, was the target of petitioners inquiring about the fate of those who disappeared during the Great Terror. By this time, most of those executed had been dead more than a decade. State-security minister S. D. Ignatiev wrote to Stalin's Politburo in October of 1951, describing how he proposed to handle the matter: [1]

> Ministry of State Security procedures have been to tell relatives of those executed that they were sentenced to ten years and sent to special regime camps without the right of correspondence. For the majority of cases, ten years have already passed, and such an answer is no longer appropriate. Without a death certificate, legal issues such as inheritance or remarriage cannot be resolved. Accordingly, relatives turn to party and judicial of-fices, to the leaders of the party and government, stubbornly insisting on conclusive answers.
>
> The Ministry of State Security proposes to establish the following rule: Relatives of those executed more than ten years earlier are to be orally told that the sentenced person died in the place of confinement. . . . If necessary a death certificate can be issued.
>
> To maintain secrecy, the lists of those sentenced to death will be main-tained in the central office and responsible state-security employees will inform relatives at the locality.

Ignatiev's solution provided only stopgap relief from the flood of inquiries that became a torrent after Stalin's death in March of 1953. Stalin's successors were caught in a dilemma. Most had participated personally in Stalin's massacres; revelation of the scope of the Great Terror could threaten them. Also, official ideology continued (up until

1956) to present Stalin and the Politburo as omniscient and flawless. To come clean about Stalin's crimes would raise fundamental questions about the nature of the communist regime.

After a three-year power struggle from which Nikita Khrushchev (himself a notorious executioner under Stalin) emerged victorious, it was decided to reveal some of the truth to the party faithful at the Twentieth Party Congress of February 1956. Khrushchev's "secret speech," which did not remain secret for long, focused only on Stalin's purge of party leaders; he scarcely mentioned the massive killing and imprisonments of ordinary citizens. Khrushchev's anti-Stalin speech unleashed a violent reaction in the Eastern European satellite countries, the most prominent being the Hungarian revolution of 1956.

It fell to Stalin's successors to decide what to do with the inquiries concerning the fate of relatives pouring into state offices. On February 10, 1956, the head of the letters department of the Council of Ministers complained to the head of state, Nikolai Bulganin, about "letters from citizens with complaints about the organs of state security which are either not answering questions about the fate of relatives arrested in 1937–1938 or are giving contradictory answers." Bulganin requested of KGB head I. Serov an explanation of current KGB procedures. The KGB's top secret response (two copies only) on April 5, 1956, less than two months after Khrushchev's secret speech, shows that Stalin's successors were still not ready to come clean:

> The answer given to relatives inquiring about the fate of relatives sentenced to death by former troikas of the OGPU or NKVD, by Special Assemblies of the NKVD-MVD, and by Military Collegiums of the Supreme Court was, until September 1955, that they were "sentenced to ten years in prison without right of correspondence and that their location was not known." Such answers, naturally, did not satisfy and led to repeated complaints and petitions. For this reason, we discussed on June 19, 1954, and on August 13, 1955, changes in the procedure for examining such requests and giving more specific answers. The Central Committee also discussed on June 19, 1954, and August 13, 1955, whether to change the procedure and to give more direct answers. On August 13, 1955, it was decided that the KGB, in consultation with the prosecutor's office, come up with recommendations on this issue.

Поэтъ Н. С. Гумилевъ, его жена поэтесса Анна Ахматова
и ихъ сынъ Левушка
(Къ 10-лѣтію разстрѣла Н. С. Гумилева большевиками.
См. на 40й стр. статью Петра Пильскаго.)

Photograph of poet Anna Akhmatova and family, including
repressed son (Lev) as a boy.

On the basis of the decision by the KGB of August 24, 1955, an instruction was issued that local KGB offices tell relatives of those sentenced to death that they were sentenced to ten years and died in captivity. In necessary cases, the death can be registered and a death certificate issued.[2]

The new KGB procedure meant that death certificates had to be issued with a false date of death. To perpetuate the lie that relatives had not been executed but had died in prison meant that dates of death had to be moved. Serov's memo gives an example of a death that was officially moved to 1942:

THE POEMS OF ANNA AKHMATOVA

> Nor in the park by the hallowed tree
> Where an inconsolable shade seeks me,
>
> But here where three hundred hours and more
> I stood and no one unlocked the door.
>
> Because even in blessed death I'm afraid
> I'll forget the noise Black Marias made
>
> And the ugly way the door slammed shut
> And the old woman's howl like a beast that was hurt.
>
> And from my motionless bronze lids
> May the thawing snow stream down like tears
>
> And the prison dove coo from afar
> And the boats go quietly down the Neva.
>
> *1940*
> *March*

(ABOVE) Anna Akhmatova's *Requiem* (English translation), describing her efforts to learn the fate of her repressed son.

(LEFT) Portrait photograph of Anna Akhmatova.

As to the inquiry of N. P. Novak, submitted to the KGB office of Denpro-
petrovsk on December 24, 1955, she received within ten days confirma-
tion of the death certificate of P. P. Novak for January 21, 1942.

Information and Rehabilitation

The flood of inquiries placed the KGB, the prosecutor, the Politburo,
and the state in an uncomfortable position. Between 1937 and 1938,
almost three quarters of a million persons were executed and their
relatives were not informed. Most had been sentenced not by courts
or tribunals but by troikas, which automatically confirmed the sentence recommended by NKVD operational groups. Between 1940 and
1955, another quarter million were executed, sentenced by military
tribunals and special assemblies. Again, their relatives were not told.

As Stalin's successors grappled with the issue, they were unable to
admit to relatives and hence to the public, that more than one million
citizens had been killed on their watch as Stalin subordinates. The
most convenient solution was to lie. Relatives were falsely told that,
if the term of the supposed prison sentence had passed, their relative
had died in prison. If the term had not yet expired, they were told that
their relative was in prison—a lie that became less credible with the
passage of time. The highest party authorities even tolerated falsifica-
tion of official records. Rather than tell the truth, they simply changed
dates of death.

Khrushchev's secret speech of February 1956 told the party faithful that most of the party members purged by Stalin were innocent.
Therefore, it was easier for the relatives of the elite to rehabilitate
their loved ones than for ordinary people. Another obstacle was that
the bureaucratic process of rehabilitating the more than one million
people executed would be overwhelming. However, there was little
doubt in official circles about the innocence of the vast majority of
those killed. A December 1953 memo from interior minister Kruglov
and chief prosecutor Rudnenko to Khrushchev stated that most of the
442,531 persons sentenced by NKVD Special Assemblies for counter-
revolutionary crimes were falsely accused, sometimes "with the most
crude violations of Soviet laws." Kruglov and Rudnenko recommended
the creation of a special commission (including themselves plus the
chairman of the supreme court and the head of a Central Committee

department) to examine cases of those incorrectly sentenced, but they conveniently decided to consider only cases after June of 1945, when death sentences averaged "only" around 3,000 per year.[3]

Relatives did not have the legal right to information on the fate of loved ones until the June 6, 1992, law of the Russian Federation "About the rehabilitation of victims of political repression" which gave rehabilitated persons, or in the case of their death, their relatives, "the right to obtain for their examination copies of the case materials" from either the interior ministry or the prosecutor's office.

Although the Russian Federation has not published official statistics of the number of executions for political offenses, it has not prevented formerly secret statistics from being published in the scientific literature.[4] Even more remarkable is the fact that the KGB's successor has posted statistics on arrests during the Stalin period on its own website.[5]

Chapter Eight

The Ship of Philosophers

Background

On the morning of September 28, 1922, the German steamer *The Oberbuergermeister Hacken* set sail from Petrograd. Its passengers included the cream of Russian intellectual life—writers, poets, journalists, scientists, and philosophers. The best known of them, philosopher Nikolai Berdiaev, strolled the deck in his broad hat and galoshes, holding a thick cane. He and other passengers were given a "Golden Book" to sign to memorialize the famous Russians traveling on the ship. On the book's cover was a picture of bass Fedor Shaliapin, a passenger on the previous voyage.

This "Ship of Philosophers" was carrying Russian intellectuals banished by the Bolsheviks from Russia. They had been arrested, investigated, and sentenced as enemies by the secret police, then called the OGPU. Most, like Berdiaev, would never see Russia again.

This is the story of the Bolsheviks' repression of intellectuals. It began in May of 1922 as one of Lenin's last major acts shortly before a first stroke that left him partially paralyzed. No longer able to speak after his third stroke in March of 1923, Lenin retired from active politics, but his anti-intellectual policies continued unabated. Lenin's May 1922 initiative resulted in the exile, imprisonment, and internal banishment of hundreds of leading intellectuals, representative of the "Silver Age" of Russian intellectual life. Under Stalin, the policy continued but was applied to a much larger numbers of intellectuals and specialists in the late 1920s and, even more broadly, during the Great Purge of 1937 to 1938.

Lenin is often portrayed sympathetically as a leader who was willing to tolerate open discussion and debate, leading to speculation that the Soviet Union would have developed a more humane form of socialism had Lenin lived. Lenin's writings took contradictory positions as he maneuvered the Bolsheviks through the civil war and the New Economic Policy introduced in March of 1921. Lenin, however, was consistent on "democratic centralism," the principle that power should be concentrated in a monopoly communist party that was only "democratic" in the sense that the party made its decisions by votes of party leaders.

This chapter shows the stark distinction between Lenin's democratic centralism, which allows some discussion within the party, and democracy, which allows open discussion among members of society at large, including intellectuals. The story begins with Lenin's repression of "non-communist" physicians and then moves to his purge of intellectuals. These purges took place during the "liberal" New Economic Policy period, and they show that the Bolsheviks could not tolerate any type of independent assembly or thinking.

Lenin: Learning How to Purge

Lenin's purge of anti-Soviet intellectuals was sparked by a letter from the minister of health (since 1918), N. A. Semashko. Semashko, himself a physician, was upset by the "anti-Soviet" attitude of the Congress of Physicians in May of 1922, prompting him to send, on May 23, 1922, the following letter to Lenin:

> To Comrade Lenin and Members of the Politburo:
>
> Respected comrades. The recent All-Russian Conference of Physicians took such a significant and dangerous turn that I consider it necessary to inform you about tactics being used with success by Kadets, Monarchists, and Social Revolutionaries [three opposition parties]. My information suggests this tendency is wide-spread not only among doctors but among other specialists (agronomists, engineers, technicians and lawyers). Even responsible persons do not recognize the danger.

What went on at the Congress can be summarized as follows: 1. A movement against Soviet medicine, 2. The demand for "freely" elected officials and grassroots independent organizations (an exact resolution of the Congress) according to formulations advanced by Kadets, Monarchists, and Social Revolutionaries, 3. A clear intent to remain outside the professional worker movement, and, 4. An intent to organize independent publishing organizations.

Semashko proposed limiting the independence of professional organizations, banning independent publishing, and imposing the obligation to practice "Soviet" medicine. He ends his letter to Lenin: "The removal of those Monarchist and Social Revolutionary doctors [gives their names] making presentations from positions of leadership should be agreed with the OGPU." In other words, the offending "anti-Soviet" physicians were to be dealt with by the secret police.

Lenin directed the letter to Stalin, who, in his position as General Secretary of the Central Committee, submitted it to the Politburo. Lenin's handwritten "question" for the Politburo reads:

> Comrade Stalin. I believe it necessary to show this letter to Dzerzhinskii [the head of the OGPU] with extreme secrecy (no copies) and to all members of the Politburo and to prepare a directive: "To direct Dzerzhinskii's OGPU to work out measures with the assistance of Semashko and to report to the Politburo (two-week deadline?)"

Stalin submitted Lenin's proposal for a Politburo vote (for repression of physicians) on the same day. Lenin's proposal, which opened the door for the suppression of any type of independent thinking or inquiry, received approval from all Politburo members (Stalin, Leon Trotsky, Lev Kamenev, Aleksei Rykov, and V. M. Molotov) except the handwritten abstention from Mikhail Tomskii (the trade union head): "I withhold my vote because the issue of the Congress of Physicians needs to be presented in a different framework. We are guilty ourselves for much of this and Semashko is the most guilty."

Following the Politburo decree, Dzerzhinskii submitted to the Politburo (within the required two-week period) his OGPU report "About Anti-Soviet Groupings Among the Intelligentsia," which identified a wide range of "anti-Soviet activities in professional organizations,

Poster of Lenin sweeping away marginals and former people, entitled
"Lenin purges the land of the unclean."

universities, scientific societies, administrative conferences, and in trusts, cooperatives, and trade organizations."[1]

On the basis of Dzerzhinskii's report, the Politburo issued a "Decree About Anti-Soviet Groupings Among the Intelligentsia" of June 8, 1922, which called for "filtering" incoming university students with strict limits on non-proletarians and checks of political reliability, restrictions of meetings of students and of professors, and bans on independent publishing activities. These checks were to be carried out by the OGPU, the personnel administrations of the higher education ministry, and the political department of the state publishing office.

The June 8, 1922, Politburo decree created a special "conference" comprised of representatives of the ministry of foreign affairs and justice department empowered "to exile abroad or to points within Russia, if a more stern punishment is not required." A commission comprised of a Politburo member (Kamenev), a ranking OGPU official (Unshlikht), and a high official of the revolutionary-military tribunal (Kurskii) was to do the final review of the list of leaders of hostile intellectual groups to be punished and the list of publishing operations to be closed.

What started as an operation against "non-communist" physicians broadened into a general witch hunt against intellectuals and professionals.

The Politburo received the list of offending physicians on June 22. It took until July 20 for the special conference to submit the names of anti-Soviet intellectuals, but the Politburo declared its work "unsatisfactory because of the small size of the list and insufficient substantiation." On the same day, Stalin received an urgent request from the OGPU to speed things up because word of impending arrests was circulating both within the country and in émigré circles.[2] A list of 186 names of anti-Soviet intellectuals was submitted on August 2, 1922, by the OGPU representative, apparently based upon a selection committee meeting of July 22. They were scheduled for arrest and then were to be deported.

The list of 186 doctors, engineers, professors, and literary figures does not follow a uniform format. The most complete cases give the name and address, the charge, and the vote of the commission, often based upon the recommendation of the personnel department of the organization for which the person worked. The sentence, in the majority of cases, was exile abroad, although a number, particularly physicians, were exiled to remote regions where they were to practice medicine. In some cases, the commission decided that the person represented no danger and was not scheduled for punishment, but the name remained on the list anyway ("The commission is against exile because he is harmless"). With these few exceptions, the others were scheduled for internal or external exile. Among the names were:

No. 23 (in the list of those investigated under case 813). ABRIKOSOV, V. V.: A priest of the Roman Catholic Church in Moscow. The son of the owner of a confectionary factory. The initiator of illegal meetings of Catholics in his home for the unification of the Roman Catholic and Orthodox Churches. A close friend of the Patriarch Tikhon and the head of the Catholic congregation in Petrograd. Carry out a search and arrest and send him abroad. He lives at Prechistenskii Boulevard House 29, Apartment 3.

No. 9 (in the list of "anti-Soviet intelligentsia" in Petrograd). ZAMIATIN, E. I.: A concealed White Guardist. Author of an illegal resolution, which he presented at the House of Literature, in which he defamed Andrei Bely for his defense of the fatherland. He is fully against Soviet power in his writings. He is a close colleague of the enemy Remizov, who has already fled. Remizov is a known enemy and Zamiatin is as well. If he is sent abroad, he could become a dangerous leader. It is necessary to send him to Novgorod or Kursk; in no case can he be sent abroad.

No. 31 (in the list of agronomists and workers of cooperative enterprises). KONDRAT'EV, N. D., Professor: Noted and close collaborator of "Journal of Agricultural Economics"—an organ of anti-Soviet agronomists. A Social Revolutionary involved in the case of the "Tactical Center." Sentenced to death for participation in the "Union of Rebirth." Death sentence changed to prison. Maintains ties with Social Revolutionaries although he officially left the party. Arrest and exile abroad. The entire commission is in favor.[3]

Eight days later (August 10), the Politburo accepted the list, ordering the OGPU to arrest the most dangerous and place the others under house arrest.[4] On August 22, the ever accurate OGPU submitted a budget to Stalin for the projected cost of exiling 217 persons abroad. On August 22 and again on August 26, 1922, the OGPU sent Stalin reports on the progress of the exile campaign with statistics on arrests, exiles, and numbers held in prisons, house arrest, or released on their own recognizance after agreeing to pay the cost of exile.

Not all sentences were carried out. Kondratyev, instead of being sent abroad, was held in a prison. According to OGPU reports, of the 67 Moscow intellectuals scheduled for exile, 12 were under house arrest, 14 were in prisons, six had not been arrested, and 21 were on their own recognizance. The most active and dangerous intellectuals were exiled in convoys of six.[5]

The Story of Berdiaev

The most famous name on the list of 186 was Nikolai Berdiaev, the world renowned philosopher of mystic non-orthodox Christianity and critical philosophy, an opponent of the close link between church and state under the czars.[6] The charge against him and suggested sentence read:

> No. 55. BERDIAEV, N. A.: Close to the publishing house "Bereg." He is being investigated as part of the cases "Tactical Center" and the "Union of Rebirth." A monarchist and a Kadet of the rightist persuasion. A member of the Black Hundred, inclined to religion, taking part in the religious counter revolution. Ionov and Poliansky are for internal exile. The Commission with the participation of Bogdanov and others is for foreign exile.

Berdiaev's story has been reconstructed from his case file and is representative of what happened to other intellectuals.[7]

Although in the early days of Soviet power, Berdiaev was allowed to continue to teach at Moscow University and to gather intellectuals in his Free Academy of Religious Culture, he was closely watched by the secret police. On February 18, 1922, Berdiaev was forced to haul scrap metal in freezing weather but was arrested after one day of work. His apartment was thoroughly searched and his manuscripts and correspondence confiscated, although he freely admitted to the arresting officer that he was an "ideological opponent of the idealization of communism." Berdiaev's arrest was based on the information of an informant (who got his name wrong), that he was a member of the "Council of Social Activists."

Berdiaev's imprisonment ended after a nocturnal interrogation by none other than the OGPU head Dzerzhinskii, his deputy Menzhinskii, and Politburo member Kamenev. In his memoirs, Berdiaev describes Dzerzhinskii: "He gave the impression of a dedicated and honest person. He was a fanatic. There was something terrifying about him. Earlier he wanted to be a Catholic monk but he transferred his fanaticism to communism." After a lengthy conversation, Dzerzhinskii told him he was free to go but that he could not leave Moscow without permission.

On August 16, Berdiaev was awakened by the OGPU's knock on his Moscow apartment door. The OGPU detachment searched his apartment from one o'clock to five o'clock A.M. and then took Berdiaev to its Lubianka headquarters. In his interrogations, Berdiaev did not hide his antipathy to communism: "Any class organization or party should be subordinated to the individual and to humanity." And: "No party past or present arouses any sympathy in me." The OGPU's verdict: exile abroad for anti-Soviet activity. Berdiaev refused to sign any confession, stating "I do not declare myself guilty of engaging in anti-Soviet activity and I particularly do not regard myself as guilty of engaging in counter-revolutionary activity during a period of military difficulties for Russia." After rejection of his protest of the verdict, Berdiaev was forced to sign a pledge not to return to Russia without permission and that he would pay the cost of his travel. Within a month, he was sailing to Germany on the "Ship of Philosophers." Berdiaev died in Paris in 1948, a world-renowned philosopher and historian whose major works were translated into many languages.

The Less Fortunate

The passengers on the Ship of Philosophers did not know so at the time, but they could count themselves as fortunate. Many intellectuals remaining in Russia, who refused to kowtow to the party, were eventually imprisoned in the Solovetskii Camp of Special Designation, which housed primarily political prisoners. Located on a remote northern island, the Solovetskii camp was noted for its cruelty and harsh conditions.

When the Great Terror began in 1937, the Solovetskii camp received an execution "limit" of 1,200 but the ambitious camp commander executed 1,615, mostly political prisoners. Lists of victims were prepared from inmate records and from informer reports. The Solovetskii commander, upon receiving approval of his execution protocols, executed two echelons (1116 and 509) in October and November of 1937.

An eyewitness account describes the departure of the second echelon marching in columns of four through the archway to the wharves:

> There I saw the face of Professor Florensii, there was white-bearded Professor Litvinov, holding his head high. There was Kotliarevskii (in a new leather cap) and Vanegengaim (in a black coat and a deerskin shirt). They see me and nod; their hands are occupied with their bags. Kotliarevskii tries unsuccessfully to smile. . . . More than a thousand were taken away that evening. . . . later there were terrible rumors that they had all been drowned.

The executions were duly reported to Moscow:

> To Major Garin, Deputy Department Head NKVD: I hereby report that, on the basis of the order signed by the head of the administration of the NKVD, Commissar Zakovskii of October 16, 1937, No. 189852 for the "highest measure of punishment" according to protocols No. 81, 82, 83, 84, and 85—1,116 persons have been executed. Signed: Capitan State Security, Matveev, November 10, 1937.[8]

Independent Organizations and Independent Thinkers

The first purge of intellectuals and other "anti-Soviet" thinkers set up a formal machinery for identifying those who did not agree with the Bolshevik regime. A special conference was established that could recommend anyone they felt was exhibiting signs of dissent or unlike thinking for jail or exile. The conference worked on the basis of employer records and recommendations, meaning that persons on poor terms with their colleagues or employers could be singled out. There was no legal recourse for those arrested. Their only review was by a committee headed by a Politburo member and an OGPU official.

Intellectuals were an early target of Bolshevik repression for fear that they would present an alternative view of reality, different from the "truth" enunciated in the official party line. The only real truth with respect to politics, economy, arts, and literature was supposed to be that enunciated by the party. "Soviet" artists, physicians, scientists, and poets were those who were prepared to accept the infinite wisdom of the party line. Anti-Soviet intellectuals were those who were prepared to disagree with the party line. Kondrat'ev, as an example, was an economist-statistician, who spent his career collecting economic data and relating what he felt these statistics had to say about economic reality. Berdiaev believed in the superiority of the individual over any party or state. The writer Zamiatin wrote allegories that might be critical of the Soviet system, but party authorities could not know for sure. Such intellectuals posed a formidable threat because their version of the truth differed from that of the party.

Soviet fear and hostility toward intellectuals continued until the end of the Soviet regime. The longest serving state-security chief, Yury Andropov, who headed the KGB from 1967 to 1982, was the party's chief warrior in its battle with intellectuals, such as Andrei Sakharov and Aleksandr Solzhenitsyn. Notably, Andropov's methods were the same as Dzerzhinskii's—internal and foreign exiles, harassment, the compiling of compromising materials—anything to neutralize their influence on Soviet society.[9]

Chapter Nine

Who Is the Prisoner Here?

Background

The Holocaust provided the classic image of the concentration camp guard: A cruel and sadistic SS officer impeccably dressed in black jackboots, indifferently sorting incoming Jewish prisoners for the gas chamber or work brigades. The Nazi concentration camps were basically extermination camps in which prisoners were either executed immediately or worked to death. The men and women who guarded these camps belonged to the fanatical SS-Totenkopfverbaende or were recruited (such as female guards) into associated organizations by racist appeals. In 1945, the Nazi concentration camps held around 700,000 inmates guarded by 55,000 guards.

At the time of Stalin's death in March of 1953, his concentration camps held 2.5 million prisoners. While the Nazis operated hundreds of camps, primarily in Eastern Europe, Stalin's Gulag administration operated 3,274 labor camps and colonies, 52 prisons, 120 children's work colonies, and 748 orphanages and hospitals spread throughout the vast territory of the Soviet Union. To run this empire, the Gulag administration employed 446,000 persons, of whom more than half (234,000) were in the militarized guard division.[1]

This chapter tells the story of the quarter-million guards who manned the sentry outposts, who escorted inmates to work, and who hunted them down when they escaped. Few, if any, were there for ideological reasons. Their officers were sent to the Gulag as punishment duty, and the guards were a rag-tag collection of poorly educated and poorly paid unfortunates, unlikely to have any affiliation with the party or with communist youth. The Gulag guard corps was at the bottom of the ladder of the interior ministry hierarchy. At the top were the Chekist operational workers who caught, imprisoned, and executed enemies of the Soviet state. Those who guarded them were at the bottom.

The job of these guards and their officers was not to exterminate prisoners; summary executions at the time of sentencing did that job more efficiently and saved transportation costs. Instead, their task was to maintain order and discipline in the camps, to prevent escapes, and to deliver and return prisoners to work in the industrial and mining enterprises associated with the camp.

Why Not the Best and the Brightest?

Nazi concentration camp guards tended to believe in Nazi racist ideology, worked in camps an easy train ride to Berlin, and, if not driven by ideology, had vast opportunities for corruption (through the theft of inmate belongings). Soviet Gulag guards lived thousands of miles from home in some of the world's harshest climates. Although some camps and colonies were located in central regions, the most important were dispersed in forlorn corners of the vast Soviet Union. They were built close to the vast mineral and forestry resources of the Far North, Siberia, and Kazakhstan.

Although prisons in other societies are not exactly located on prime real estate, they can scarcely compare in remoteness and hardship with the prisons of the Soviet Gulag. As a massive industrial and mining empire, the Gulag spun off a huge demand for guards in a society that was perennially short of labor. The USSR, in 1953, had a prison population fifteen times larger than the United States, a country of comparable size. The Gulag administration faced a constant struggle of recruiting and retaining guards.

In any penitentiary system, the task of guards is basically the same: All societies isolate violent and dangerous offenders as a threat to the physical safety and property of their citizens. In the Soviet case, most inmates were condemned to the Gulag not as threats to public safety but because of actual or suspected opposition to the Soviet state.

That guards perform their jobs well was extremely important to the leadership. If the guarding system broke down, civil society could be swamped with "socially dangerous" persons who could infect the rest of society with their anti-Soviet views. Yet, there was little reason to expect that Gulag guards would be the "best and the brightest." Guards had to work in remote regions where free labor would not come on its own. Guarding is a cruel, brutal, and unrewarding business in its own right, let alone in an arctic climate. Unless the Gulag administration was to pay exceptional wages and benefits, there would also be no reason for qualified persons to volunteer for guard positions.

The official statistics for the militarized guard division of the Gulag for 1945 show that only twelve percent belonged to the party, ninety percent had an elementary education or less, and almost eighty percent had been on the job less than a year.[2] If one adjusts these figures to exclude officers (who accounted for about ten percent of the total), the characteristics of ordinary guards look even worse.

Their officers were not much better. NKVD/MVD officers with uncompromised backgrounds and good training opted for careers in the central administration or in the glamorous operational administrations. The guard division was a dumping ground for compromised officers sent to Gulag camps under the motto: "You can take those whom we do not need."[3] "Officer" positions in the Gulag even had to be fulfilled by "free labor," suggesting even a shortage of officers. In 1948, 26,254 of the 63,033 officer positions were filled by "free labor."[4] Given that most camps were off limits to civilians, many of these "free" officers were either prisoners themselves or former prisoners.

That the Gulag was not a particularly desirable place of employment is reflected in the fact that of the 337,484 authorized positions in the camp sector, 21 percent were unfilled (in 1948). In the early 1930s, shortages were so severe that prisoners occupied managerial positions in camp administration. During the construction of the White Sea–Baltic Canal, most lower-level administrative and technical positions were held by prisoners. Although the Gulag administration sought to minimize the use of prisoners as guards for obvious reasons, the number of prisoner-guards was substantial. As of January 1939, of the 94,921 armed guards in camps and colonies, 25,023 were prisoners.[5] The practice of using prisoner-guards continued throughout the history of the Gulag.

The Gulag had other ways to force "free" persons into guard positions. Many inmates became guards after their sentences were completed because internal passport controls would not permit them to live elsewhere. After World War II, Red Army soldiers, POWs, displaced persons, and others who would have been in Germany or in other foreign countries were automatically processed in "filtration" camps. Many who escaped imprisonment were made into concentration camp guards. Others had their papers taken away and had no choice but to remain as guards. At the beginning of 1946, the number of such guards numbered 31,000.[6]

The sorry conditions of the armed guards of the Gulag were summarized in a letter to the NKVD minister Beriia in August of 1945:

> At the current time, most of the armed guards are older persons and war invalids. Many have asked to be demobilized based on the state decree about demobilizing older persons. The Gulag administration gives a standard answer to such requests that the personnel staff is not subject to this decree. Such an answer is correct for the present but the basic question is the future insofar as most guards are older than forty, disqualified from military service because of health, war invalids, or women. Our efforts to recruit demobilized solders is not yielding results. There are other substantive deficiencies. For example in the armed guards, we have in the commanding staff in officer ranks free workers recruited from collective farms and cities in the ordinary fashion.[7]

Although former Red Army soldiers understood weaponry, those recruited from the collective farms did not. Guards did not know how to clean their rifles, and one female guard went on duty with a rag stuffed in her rifle.[8]

Work Conditions and Discipline

Guards were poorly paid, equipped, and trained. An August 1945 report to Beriia contains the following description of Gulag guards:

The armed guards of many camps do not wear uniforms. They wear ripped shoes and tattered clothing. In the summer, they wear winter hats, wadded trousers, and quilted jackets. Their appearance is worse than that of the prisoners although the disciplinary rules of the Red Army apply to them.[9]

The proposal to Beriia: Make the armed Gulag guards a part of the NKVD Special Forces. The proposal was rejected because of the high cost and problems of mobilizing armed guards for the Gulag.[10]

Gulag guards worked long hours under generally miserable conditions in harsh climates. A March 1950 report stated that:

The work day of armed guards is excessively hard and, as a general rule, is 10 to 12 hours, and during the summer months longer. Their days off are irregular; their vacations are withheld and are granted primarily in the winter.[11]

A January 20, 1950, report to the head of the Gulag administration showed that the living conditions of guards had not improved: "In many divisions, the staff is miserly quartered, some in wagons, and some in heated huts."[12]

Gulag guards had to stand guard under freezing conditions. According to Gulag folklore, prisoners would taunt guards manning watchtowers in freezing weather from their barracks: "Who are prisoners here? You or us?"

In one instance, a guard was electrocuted when he tried to attach a primitive stove to an electrical line. When his death was investigated, it was determined that forty-three guards had jerry-rigged primitive heating devices to electrical wires at their posts "without the permission of the commander."[13]

Armed guards worked for little pay under difficult conditions, and, in many cases, they were forced into the job. It is therefore no wonder that morale and discipline were low. The Gulag administration prepared regular reports on disciplinary actions against its employees in the camp sector. On December 1, 1948, there were 276,661 employees working in the camps, the vast majority of which were guards. Of these 61,729 (22 percent) were fired or "left" in 1948. Of these, 13,003 left because of illness or age, but almost 20,000 were fired for violation of discipline, occupational crimes, etc. The report also shows that thirteen percent (36,521) of all camp employees as of 1948 had been indicted, arrested, demoted, or had reprimands placed in their records.[14]

Given the manpower shortages, those infractions that led to firing must have been very serious. Of those fired in 1948, 4,370 were fired by the central administration of the MVD.

Fraternization

Within the camp, "observers" or "operationals" had direct contact with inmates. They assigned them their tasks, monitored their whereabouts within the camp grounds, and spied. According to camp records, there were almost 140,000 "informers" among the inmates, of whom one half were to report planned escapes.[15] Contact between guards and prisoners was to be strictly limited. Armed guards manned the watchtowers and patrolled the area around the camp, they escorted prisoners to work and back, and they transported prisoners from one camp to another. Other than that, they were to have no contact. Such anti-fraternization rules were to prevent guards from exchanging information with inmates, from being "infected" by their political views, or from developing friendly relationships that might lead to assistance in escape attempts. Gulag guards were subject to a drumbeat of political education, instructing them that they were guarding vicious and dangerous enemies of the people.

One can imagine why these anti-fraternization rules would be ignored. Many guards were themselves only a step removed from being inmates themselves. A large number were former inmates who had served out their term and had no where else to go. Others had passed through filtration camps at the end of the war and had narrowly escaped imprisonment themselves. Still others had their papers confiscated and were tied to the camp. If the guards obeyed fraternization rules, they had to keep company only with other guards, and they would probably be deprived of female companionship, which they could "find" among female inmates.

Indeed, fraternization was rampant: A representative 1946 MVD report criticized the "unsatisfactory political-educational work of camp staff and cases of contacts with prisoners, group drunkenness, and hooliganism."[16] Another typical report (dated October 1941) entitled "Co-habitation of armed guards with female prisoners, drunkenness and other violations of military discipline" complained:

> Discipline among the guard staff is lax. There are cases of guards going on watch drunk, of co-habitation with women inmates. . . . The commander of the division, Shevchuk, knows about this but takes no action. In the fourth platoon, the guards Rezepov, Grishchuk and Girnev co-habit with female prisoners. A guard of this platoon, Novikov, co-habited with female prisoners Tomlina, Arkhipova, Kbardinova and Vasilieiva. When this became known in the platoon, he committed suicide. [We wonder whether the term "co-habitation" was code for rape?]. . . . Another guard of this platoon, Churkin, on October 4, 1941, guarding nine prisoners at the ZhanaArka station, left the prisoners by themselves, went to drink with a female friend and remained there until the prisoners found him themselves.[17]

The murder of two inmates by an NKVD guard in the Agrinskii Labor Camp began with fraternization that ended in a deadly argument. The incident was reported directly to the head of the Gulag administration and to the NKVD deputy minister in the following 1942 report:[18]

> In the electro station of construction site 203, the guard, Ananevy, and the prisoner, Khvatovy, argued over cigarettes. During the ensuing scuffle, Khvatovy struck Ananevy, after which the guard took a hammer and killed him with a blow to the head. Another inmate and a free worker responded to the noise. Fearing that he would be caught at the scene of the crime, Ananevy killed the second inmate with a hammer blow and seriously wounded the free worker, leaving him unconscious. As these murders were taking place, the other prisoners returned from work.

The report ends with the terse statement: "The guard was arrested and the investigation is under way." Given the high level of this report, we imagine that the guard's punishment was quite severe. The guard's major offenses were, first, the near killing of a free worker, and second, engaging in fraternization. In 1942, the killing of an inmate alone would probably not have attracted much attention.

Some fraternization reached comedic proportions: A January 2, 1951, report described a guard in the Krasnoiarsk region, "fulfilling the temporary duties of the head of a convoy, who took two prisoners with him beyond the zone of production and organized a drunken spree with them. The drunken guard gave his automatic rifle to a prisoner, who opened fire and wounded the guard in the leg." The report concludes that "such cases are not rare."[19]

The widespread practice of fraternization did not mean the absence of widespread cruelty and violence by guards against inmates. Some examples: An overseer aided by male prisoners forcibly shaved and beat female prisoners.[20] Transport guards withheld supplies from prisoners in transit, many of whom arrived at their destinations in a state of starvation. Drunken guards stole prisoner belongings, raped women prisoners, and beat prisoners for no reason. Prisoners were forced to stand freezing in the snow and were set upon by guard dogs.[21]

Prisoners as Resources

In 1953, there were 2.6 million prisoners in the Gulag's camps and colonies. They engaged in the production of minerals, and in agriculture, forestry, and construction. Although the Gulag accounted for only two percent of the labor force, it accounted for, in some cases, such as nickel and gold, up to one hundred percent of production. In construction, which was carried out in remote regions and hostile climates, Gulag prisoners accounted for up to twenty percent.

Clearly, a "rational" Gulag administration would want to preserve its most valuable resource; namely, the inmates themselves. Indeed, in 1946, the economic activities of the Gulag were transferred in large part to independent economic administrations that reported directly to the MVD. The Gulag administration was left in charge of the inmates and was no longer responsible for production goals. It also learned that it could lease out its inmates for money to the industrial ministries. At this point, the records show a change in attitudes toward prisoners. The Gulag administration started to remind camp plant managers about nutrition norms and other rules relating to worker health and safety.

In any prison setting, the welfare of inmates is as much determined by guards, wardens, and medical personnel as it is by central decrees. The business of guarding prisoners, worldwide, is far from glamorous. It is likely to attract sadists who welcome the prospect of abusing other people. Poor guard pay and hostile climatic conditions would scarcely create a favorable environment for inmates. It is therefore to be expected that Gulag guards did not perform their duties well; that they disobeyed fraternization orders; and that many of them were cruel.

In the later years of the Gulag, the weakness of the guarding system led to a breakdown. The only way camp managers could maintain order was to turn discipline over to organized gangs of prisoners who basically ran the camp. The inability of the Gulag management to maintain control of the camps, as eventually manifested in massive camp uprisings that required armed troops, was one reason for the liquidation of the camp system starting in 1953.[22]

Chapter Ten

Reasoning with Stalin on Zero Tolerance

Background

A distinctive features of Stalin's criminal justice system was its more severe punishment of theft of state and collective property than of private property. Even the most petty of thefts carried mandatory Gulag sentences. The Law of August 7, 1932, "About the Protection of Social Property," was enacted as the famine of 1932–33 was ravaging Ukraine, Kazakhstan, and parts of Russia, and it punished the theft of small amounts of grain with death sentences or ten years in the Gulag. Collective farmers who took small amounts of grain from the fields or milk from "socialist" cows found themselves toiling in the mines and timber fields of Siberia, or worse.

The "mild" Law of August 10, 1940, punished petty theft from state enterprises with only one year in prison. The harsh anti-theft law, the infamous Decree of June 4, 1947, "About criminal responsibility for theft of state and socialist property," mandated minimum sentences of five to seven years for theft of state or socialist property. Under the June 1947 decree, stealing was punished with long prison terms whether one kilogram or one ton of grain was taken. Repeat offenders, thefts organized by groups, and thefts in large quantities were punished by sentences up to twenty years.

This chapter tells the story of the implementation of the 1947 anti-theft law by a criminal justice system that eventually concluded that it was, in fact, too harsh. Justice officials tried to ameliorate the law but met with fierce resistance from Stalin. They had to await Stalin's death to get more "reasonable" sentencing laws.

The June 1947 Law: The Text

The June 1947 anti-theft law is a parsimonious decree that allows little or no room for interpretation.[1] It required minimum five- to seven-year sentences for theft of state or socialist property and made failure to report offenses subject to mandatory jail terms:

> For the purpose of creating a unified set of laws about criminal responsibility for the theft of state and socialized property and the strengthening of the battle against such crimes, the Presidium of the Supreme Soviet of the USSR decrees:
>
> 1. The theft, the appropriation, the squandering or embezzlement or any other theft of state property is to be punished with confinement in a corrective-labor institution for 7 to 10 years with or without confiscation of property.
>
> 2. The theft of state property that is committed repeatedly or by an organized group or in large magnitudes is to be punished by confinement in a corrective-labor camp for a term of 10 to 20 years with confiscation of property.

[Articles 3 and 4 apply slightly lower penalties to theft of collective or socialist property.]

> 5. Failure to report to authorities reliable information that theft of state or socialized property is being planned or has taken place as described in articles 2 and 4 of the decree is to be punished by loss of freedom of two to three years or banishment for a period of 5 to 7 years.

Prosecuting the 1947 Anti-theft Law

The 1937 anti-theft law was draconian, but there are ways for so-ciety to modify overzealous laws. Crimes must be reported, but the managers and administrators, the ones most likely to witness thefts, may not want to lose workers to prison for trivial offenses. Sentences had to be issued by local prosecutors and judges who might know the defendants or their relatives and friends. They could look for mitigat-ing circumstances; they could try to find excuses.

Stalin's criminal justice system combated such local pressures for leniency by making the mandatory sentences unequivocal, by moni-toring judges and prosecutors (even punishing soft justice officials), and by making non-reporting a crime in itself.

The justice ministry was responsible for the conduct of its judges. The primary message of justice ministry reports was that the citi-zenry could rest easy because the justice ministry was vigilant: "The Ministry of Justice is undertaking all necessary measures to eliminate defects in the work of judges in applying the Decree of June 4, 1947." Its regular reports brag to Stalin about the forceful "battle against theft."

Such pride was justified. A remarkable half million people were prosecuted in the remaining seven months of 1947 after the June law was enacted. Thereafter, justice ministry reports heralded "successes" as evidenced by the declining but still high number of convictions for theft, which stood at a quarter million convictions in both 1948 and 1949. Despite these achievements, the record was not perfect. Justice ministry statistics show that, of those sentenced under the June 4, 1947, decree, six percent received less than five years and some even received suspended sentences—evoking the following complaint about local judges and prosecutors from the justice ministry:

> In the practice of applying the [June 4, 1947] Decree, judges make a large number of mistakes and distortions that weaken the struggle against the theft of state and socialist property: There are unsubstantiated sentences by judges, unfounded deviations from penalties called for by the Decree, the unfounded usage of conditional sentences, and also foot-dragging in investigations. In addition, the prosecutor and police, in many cases, do

Poster of Stalin with a happy group of collective farmers (many of whom were punished for petty thefts from the fields under his anti-theft campaigns).

not "arrest" the property of the accused, giving the thief an opportunity to conceal the stolen property.[2]

Judges could be too lenient, but they could also make mistakes: "Investigatory agencies often bring unfounded indictments for criminal acts, which mean that citizens are unfairly prosecuted and sentenced." Thus, the tough judge could be accused of convicting innocent citizens, and the lenient judge accused of deviating from the punishments set by the Great Stalin himself.

Trying to Soften Up Stalin

Stalin's top administrators reached their lofty positions by being able to anticipate his wishes and thinking. If they lacked this skill, they quickly disappeared from positions of authority. His top justice officials applied incessant pressure on prosecutors and judges to strictly follow the mandatory sentencing guidelines, even threatening lenient judges and soft republics (such as Ukraine) with repercussions.

By 1951, Stalin's leading justice officials had seen more than a million people sentenced to more than five years, often for the pettiest of thefts; any sentence in excess of three years meant automatic incarceration in a camp of the Gulag. The three top criminal justice officials—the minister of justice (K. Gorshenin), the USSR Prosecutor (G. Safonov), and the chairman of the Supreme Court (A. Volin)—thought the time was ripe for a "softer" approach to theft. Presumably these were no amateurs with respect to dealing with Stalin.

In a rather remarkable cooperative effort, these three top justice officials decided in April of 1951 to try to budge Stalin from his zero tolerance policy on petty theft of state and socialist property. On or around April 24, 1951, the trio authored a joint "secret" letter to Stalin entitled "About some misuses of the application of the Decree of June 4, 1947," which contained a draft decree for Stalin to sign: "About criminal responsibility for theft of state and socialized property to persons committing petty, insignificant theft" to reduce sentences for petty first-time thefts.[3]

Their joint letter shows their strategy to convince the old man (at that time Stalin had less than two years to live) that it was time for moderation. They begin by reaffirming the wisdom of Stalin's June 1947 decree and assuring him that it was being implemented without "deviations":

> To Comrade Stalin, I.V.:
>
> The passage of the Decree of June 4, 1947, "About criminal responsibility for the theft of state and socialized property" along with other measures has significantly strengthened work against theft and embezzlement. Prosecutorial agencies are bringing such thieves of socialized property to their criminal responsibility without deviations and judges are sentencing them according to the Decree of June 4, 1947, to the harshest measures of punishment.

They then build their case for amelioration in the case of petty theft by first-time offenders:

However, in addition to thieves, who cause significant losses to the state through their crimes, there are a substantial number brought to their criminal responsibility by the Decree of June 4, 1947, committing for the first time small, insignificant acts of thievery. These persons are also sentenced for long terms insofar as the Decree of June 4, 1947, calls for minimal terms of punishment for theft of state property with the loss of freedom for 7 years, for socialized property 5 years.

To bring their case home, the troika of justice officials cites extreme cases that show the need for amendment of the law:

Frequently, women with young children, war invalids, and youths are being sentenced to long terms of confinement. For example, Golovenkina, a female worker at Makhachkala port was sentenced to 10 years for the theft of two kilograms of wheat. Invalid of the Patriotic War of Group II Nasushchnyi, awarded state medals, was sentenced to 7 years for the theft from the bakery where he worked of 2 kilograms of bread. Transport worker Iurina, whose husband was killed at the front and who was left with a 12-year-old child, was sentenced to 7 years for the theft of one kilogram of rice. Female worker Martynes was sentenced to 7 years for the theft from her dormitory of bed sheets. Transport worker Grabo, a wounded veteran of the Patriotic War, was sentenced to 7 years confinement for the theft of 7 packages of cigarettes. The 68-year-old Kolkhoz worker Kamalova was sentenced to 7 years for the theft on July 5 of 5 kilograms of rye, which were taken from him when he was held. The student at the FZO school Khorzhevskii was sentenced to 7 years for the theft of 2 kilograms of potatoes from the school's private plot.

Having set up their argument, the troika submits its compromise proposal: to use the earlier law of 1940—also zero tolerance but only one-year sentences for petty theft and first-time offenders—in place of the harsh June 1947 law:

The Supreme Court in its capacity as overseer makes corrections in specific cases of excessively harsh punishment, but this does not solve the problem. Before the Decree of June 4, 1947, the Decree of August 10, 1940, was in effect, which required a minimum sentence of confinement of one year for petty theft, at the place of work, irrespective of its magnitude. When the Decree of June 4, 1947, was published, the Plenum of the Supreme Court of the USSR on August 22, 1947, issued instructions to courts to use the exact measures of punishment called for in the Decree. Despite the necessity to strengthen the battle against theft of socialist property, we propose that the June 4, 1947, measures of punishment not be applied to first-time offenders committing petty, insignificant thefts. We consider it correct to apply in such cases the Decree of August 10, 1940, which calls for a prison term of one year. We present herewith for approval a draft of a decree of the Plenum of the Supreme Court of the USSR. Signed: Minister of Justice USSR, K. GORSHENIN, General Prosecutor USSR, G. SAFONOV, Chairman of Supreme Court USSR, A. VOLIN

Stalin Stands Firm and Why

Stalin's three highest justice officials recommended that petty thieves be sentenced to one year in jail for first-time offenses—a seemingly reasonable position. Their draft decree entitled "About mistakes in the implementation of the Decree of June 4, 1947" was submitted to the administrative department of the Central Committee in the hope (expectation) that Stalin would sign off.

There is no further record of this decree in the Central Committee archives. It disappears from view, which was Stalin's way of rejecting proposals he did not like. Sentencing statistics confirm that Stalin held firm to the long jail sentences. Stalin was not prepared to show mercy to petty offenders, no matter how overwhelming the advice.

Why was Stalin not willing to bend? It may be that Stalin understood the consequences of unchallenged petty theft at the place of work or in agricultural fields. With property belonging to the state or to the collective farm, the products produced there belonged "to everyone and hence to no one." If a few people stole a few kilograms of grain from the fields or radios from the factory, there would be no great harm. But if everyone stole, even small amounts, the harm to the state could be considerable. Moreover, with everyone either stealing or thinking about stealing, the only way to frighten off the millions of potential thieves would be by exacting excessive punishments even for small crimes.

Stalin's successors wasted little time in softening the June 1947 law. In a 1955 proposal to the Supreme Court, the director of the department for examining pardons proposed to set a maximum sentence for theft at ten years, citing cases where persons were sentenced to more than ten years for relatively minor thefts:

> Sentencing to long periods of confinement (15–25 years) complicates the fulfillment of the most basic task of criminal justice—the reeducation of criminals. In many cases, the criminal loses sight of the perspective of being freed and falls under the influence of organized criminal gangs and, instead of correcting himself, carries out new crimes. Long prison terms, as a rule, destroy the family because according to existing laws a sentence of more than three years is a formal grounds for divorce.[4]

The post-Stalin leadership, therefore, considered law enforcement as a correctional system designed to rehabilitate the criminal, versus Stalin's view of it as a system to protect the state. In effect, Stalin's successors entered a new social compact with their citizenry. The new leadership overlooked minor infractions like petty theft and poor work performance that, under Stalin, were punished by prison. This new social compact was pithily captured by the motto: "We pretend to work and you pretend to pay us"; that is, we'll ignore the faults and mistakes of the leaders if they ignore our own.

Chapter Eleven

Bolshevik Discourse

Before and After

Background

Until Lenin's death in January of 1924, the highest ruling body, the Politburo, operated on the principle of "democratic centralism." The key economic, political, and military decisions were to be made by the Politburo, but, within the Politburo, members could freely express their opinion. Once a Politburo majority or consensus was formed, however, Politburo members had to fall in line and support the decision.

Lenin's death without a designated successor set off a fierce power struggle from which an unlikely Politburo member, Joseph Stalin, emerged victorious. Stalin, who others underestimated as a dull party bureaucrat, used his position as party general secretary to set Politburo agendas and to control administrative appointments. Stalin's use of these bureaucratic levers allowed him to place his people in key party positions for working majorities in the Politburo and Central Committee. After removal of visible political opponents, the Politburo was left with Stalin loyalists, who had few independent thoughts of their own. At this point (around December of 1930), Stalin pretty much had his way within the Politburo, and by the mid-1930s no one dared to challenge him.

This chapter tells the tale of the demise of democratic centralism as Stalin consolidated his power. Once Stalin was, as his colleagues would later call him, "master of the house," he dictated the "unified party line" which other Bolshevik leaders automatically supported and adopted as their own. With Stalin dictating policy, no room was left for discussion or dissent. In fact, even the slightest "deviation" from Stalin's unified party line came to be interpreted as "factionalism" or, even worse, as a crime against the state.

Two snapshots of Politburo meetings—the first from September 8, 1927, and the second of November 22, 1932—tell the tale of the slide from open Politburo discussion. In the September 1927 session, Stalin's Politburo majority (which included his later victims Prime Minister Aleksei Rykov and Pravda editor Nikolai Bukharin) fought against the potent "united opposition" of Leon Trotsky, Lev Kamenev, and Grigory Zinovyev. In this fateful meeting, the United Opposition demanded that its own platform be presented to the upcoming party congress as an alternative to Stalin's program. The discussion, as of September 1927, was open, frank, vitriolic, and profane as the two sides fought tooth and nail. Stalin's side, as usual, won the day.

In the Politburo meeting of November 22, 1932, several mid-level party members stood accused of criticizing Stalin in private meetings in their apartments, dachas, on vacation, and at drinking parties. One of them, A. P. Smirnov, was an Old Bolshevik—a member of the Central Committee and deputy chair of the Russian Republic Government. Another purported critic was N. B. Eismont, deputy minister of trade for the Russian Republic. Their critical remarks had been reported to Stalin by two informants, longstanding members of the party Nikolskii and Savelev. The November 22, 1932, meeting was called to discuss the "treachery" of Smirnov and Eismont.

The Transcripts of Politburo Meetings

Until Stalin's consolidation of power, there were regular meetings of the Politburo. Although there was a requirement adopted in 1923 that verbatim transcripts of the major agenda items were to be kept, few transcripts were actually prepared, and only thirty-one are preserved. They have been published as *Stenograms of the Politburo of the Communist Party* in Russian as a joint project of the Hoover Institution and the Russian Archival Service[1] along with an analysis of these transcripts, *The Lost Transcripts of the Politburo,* in English.[2]

Stenographic accounts were taken of Politburo meetings at the request of Politburo members. After Stalin's consolidation of power, they were made only when he so decided. Before his ascendancy, any member of the Politburo could request such a transcript. Those in the minority often requested a transcript to have a written record of speeches and remarks.

Politburo stenographic accounts were made to inform the party about Politburo decisions. After the meeting, each speaker was given a copy of his remarks for editing. Thereafter, the edited version of the meeting was bound in red-covered pamphlets for distribution to the party's Central Committee members or to an even broader group. These red pamphlets gave party members their marching orders with respect to the latest twists and turns in party policy.

Transcripts of Politburo meetings whose contents were judged too sensitive (such as revealing wide splits within the party leadership) were not distributed or were limited to a select few party leaders. The transcript of the September 8, 1927 meeting was prepared for distribution but then withheld as too sensitive. Stalin insisted on preparing the transcripts of the November 22, 1932, meeting to send the word to party members that not the slightest criticism of his policies was to be permitted.

No Holds Barred: Stalin Versus Trotsky, September 8, 1927

The denouement of the struggle of the "United Opposition" headed by Leon Trotsky, Grigory Zinovyev, and Lev Kamenev against the Politburo majority headed by Stalin, Nikolai Bukharin, and Aleksei Rykov, survives in a verbatim account of the proceedings of September 8, 1927. At the time of this meeting, Trotsky, Kamenev, and Zinovyev were no longer members of the Politburo (Kamenev had been demoted to candidate member; the others excluded). The most severe sanction lay ahead of them: They were expelled from the party in November and December of 1927. Kamenev and Zinovyev were executed in the first Moscow Show Trial in 1936. Trotsky was executed in Mexico by an assassin sent by Stalin in 1940.

The issue being debated was the opposition's demand that its alternative platform be published and sent out to party members in preparation for the upcoming party congress. The opposition cited the Politburo under Lenin, when, they claimed, alternative views

Sketches of the United Opposition:
(TOP) Leon Trotsky,
(CENTER) Grigory Zinovyev,
(BOTTOM) Lev Kamenev.

could be freely expressed. The ruling majority, on the other hand, rejected the publication of the opposition platform, citing formal party rules on timetables and the fact that an alternative program would create a second party and destroy the "existing dictatorship of the proletariat." Stalin, as the general secretary of the Central Committee, controlled the agenda. In this case, he invited allies from the Central Control Commission to overwhelm the outgunned Trotsky, Kamenev, and Zinovyev.

The short excerpt from the seventy-one page transcript shows Stalin's mastery of bureaucratic detail, his debating skills, and the vituperative atmosphere that existed within the Politburo at this time. It also shows Stalin's practice of speaking not for himself but for the "workers" that he represented. Stalin's opponents employ all their heavy weapons: They accuse him of incompetence as a civil war military leader, and they even cite Lenin's "Political Testament" in which he recommends Stalin's removal. Their most general charge is that Stalin has stifled discussion within the party and will not let alternate views be expressed. Stalin's response is that the Politburo and Central Committee (which he controls) are the party, and "the party," not individuals, decides what is to be presented to the party membership for discussion. The meeting ends with resolutions barring the opposition from distributing its platform or from having contacts with foreign communists who might publicize their ideas.

The excerpts begin after a rather lengthy statement by Stalin defending himself from opposition charges of incompetence during the civil war. The chairman is Stalin ally Ian Rudzutak.[3]

CHAIRMAN: Comrade Stalin, your time has run out.

VOICES: Extend his time.

TROTSKY: Give him another five minutes.

CHAIRMAN: Are there objections?

TROTSKY: Of course not, let him speak.

STALIN: Comrade Trotsky demands equality between the Central Committee, which carries out the decisions of the party, and the opposition, which undermines these decisions. A strange business! In the name of what organization do you have the audacity to speak so insolently with the party?

ZINOVYEV: Each member of the party has the right to speak before the party congress, and not only organizations.

STALIN: I think that it is not permitted to speak so insolently as a turncoat to the party.

ZINOVYEV: Don't try to split us; don't threaten.

STALIN: You are splitting yourselves off. This is your misfortune. The combined plenum of the Central Committee and Central Control Commission ruled to allow open discussion a month before the congress [only] after publication of the theses of the Central Committee. Why do Trotsky and Zinovyev remain silent on this point? They want to violate the decision of the combined plenum and open discussion three months before the congress! Is it really difficult to understand that the Central Committee will not take this anti-party step, that the Central Committee will honor the decision of the combined plenum as well as the resolution of the tenth and thirteenth congresses about the rules of discussion of the platform?

They talk about Bonapartism. What is Bonapartism? It is the attempt of the minority to subject the majority to its will by force. Who, besides eccentrics, could assert that the majority of our party binds itself to its will by way of force? Surely that is stupid. If there is a possible effort at Bonapartism, that can only come from the side of the opposition, because it represents an insignificant minority, and probably will not have one delegate at the party congress.

TROTSKY: Evidently [ironically, meaning Stalin will make sure of that].

STALIN: ... They scorn us, saying that we are afraid of the truth, that we are against free discussion. This is nonsense, Comrades. Look at the stenograms of the combined plenum. There are three editions, about one thousand pages. We distributed 8,000 copies. There are the speeches of the defenders of the party line and of its opponents. The workers have the opportunity to compare and make their decision. Where is the fear of the truth? And what has the opposition offered that is new in its so-called "platform" in addition to its speeches in these stenograms? Absolutely nothing new! Why do they insist on new discussions? Because they want to disorganize the party, to prevent us from carrying out positive work and to create the impression that the party is unstable. But we cannot deprive ourselves of positive work for the sake of the whims of the opposition. Maybe, for the opposition, positive work represents an unnecessary luxury, but we can't allow the harmful illusion that the party is turning into a discussion club, that the party is unstable and so on. We cannot do this, first, because it does not correspond to reality, second, it contradicts our conception of the party, and third, we are surrounded by armed enemies. And then, the opposition has the crazy idea to write a lengthy brochure, and they want us to respond, so that this battle becomes known abroad and creates the impression of weakness in our party.

TROTSKY: Those from *Pravda* know that there is only a pretense of discussion.

STALIN: They say that under Lenin there was a different regime, that under Lenin they did not send away the opposition, did not deport them, etc. You have a weak memory, Comrades from the opposition. Don't you remember that Lenin proposed to send Comrade Trotsky to the Ukraine? Comrade Zinovyev, is this true or not? Why are you silent?

ZINOVYEV: I am not under interrogation by you (laughter, bell of the chairman).

TROTSKY [playing his trump card]: And you hide Lenin's "testament"? Lenin in his "testament" revealed everything about Stalin. Stalin is completely revealed. There is nothing to add or subtract.

STALIN: You lie if you assert that anyone is concealing the "testament" of Lenin. You know well that it is known to all the party. You know also, as does all the party, that Lenin's testament demolishes exactly you, the current leader of the opposition. . . . Further, is it not true that under Lenin Comrades Tomsky and Sokol'nikov were sent away to other regions, to Turkistan and to other places? True or not? Is it true or not that Lenin in such a decisive moment as the October Revolution demanded the expulsion of Comrades Zinovyev and Kamenev from the party? Is this a fact or not? What does this all tell us? It tells us that Lenin recognized the necessity of repression no better or worse than the Central Committee of our party. Judge now the value of your idle chatter about the regime of the party.

. . . And the opposition demands that we publish these and other such defamations of the party. Consider what would happen if we really did publish them. The bourgeoisie of the West, learning of Trotsky and Zinovyev's false statement that our party is ready for any and every concession, will pressure us even more . . . [repetition eliminated, author] . . . and we will not be able delay war for even a few years. Such is the likely result of opposition demagoguery if their vile defamation is published. Is it really possible for such people to speak about our party in such a fashion without appearing as enemies of our party and government?

ZINOVYEV: If you say we are Chamberlain's agents, does this help our government or Chamberlain? Of course, it helps Chamberlain [British prime minister].

STALIN: No one called you an agent of Chamberlain, but understand how blinded you have become in your factional struggle. But understand to what degree you have lost your sight in your factional struggle, the degree to which you have shut yourself in your sorry factional shell, the degree to which you have lost your heads in your battle against the party that you are prepared to write a false denunciation of the party. Is it possible for a member of the party to speak against his own proletarian government, to falsely denounce the party, the government? . . . Only those who have joined the camp of our enemies could go so far. But we wish to pull you out of this dead end . . .

TROTSKY: You should pull your own self out of the swamp first. (Noise, shouting, the bell of the chairman.)

ZINOVYEV: You should get out of the dead end yourself. We are on Lenin's road, and you have left it.

STALIN: Allow yourself to scandalmonger, Comrade Zinovyev. You cannot escape from these decisions of the Comintern and the party. And people such as you demand that we publish their anti-party, scandalous, and false denunciation of our party for the benefit of capitalism, making our international position more difficult. Is it not clear that you have gone mad, demanding from us the impossible? Is it not clear that after this, the platform of the opposition is the platform of complete intellectual and political bankruptcy of petty bourgeois intellectuals gone wild?

CHAIRMAN: Comrade Iaroslavskii has the floor.

TROTSKY: Comrade Stalin spoke 25 minutes.

CHAIRMAN: Exactly 20 minutes.

TROTSKY: Comrade Stalin spoke 24 minutes.

CHAIRMAN: Your watch must be more reliable than the sun. Comrade Iaroslavskii has the floor.

Keep Quiet and Survive

The November 27, 1932, Politburo session is in marked contrast to the no-holds-barred September 1927 meeting. Whereas in September of 1927, Trotsky, Kamenev, and Zinovyev were prepared to levy the most serious charges against Stalin in the most unrestrained language, the November 27, 1932, session was called to condemn criticism of Stalin, made in private conversations behind closed doors. To speak ill of Stalin even in private had become a crime against the state.

The Politburo session was called after denunciations and the interrogations of several mid-level party officials (N. B. Eismont, the head of trade of the Russian Republic and V. N. Tolmachev, a former head of the Russian Republic interior ministry), which implicated a member of the Central Committee, A. P. Smirnov, who was called to the meeting to defend himself.

They were charged with forming an "illegal faction" in informal meetings in private apartments or dachas, during which Stalin's industrialization and collectivization programs were questioned. Accusations of "illegal meetings and illegal discussions" were submitted to the Central Committee (probably by Stalin himself), and the accused (Eismont and Tolmachev) were interrogated by the OGPU. The accused characterized these meetings as purely social and suggested that many of them were drunk at the time. Private or not, repeated or not, drunk or not, the Politburo's decision was that such meetings constituted the formation of an "anti-party group." Eismont and Tolmachev were expelled from the party, and their cases were turned over to the OGPU. Smirnov's case was sent for further investigation by the Politburo.

Smirnov and Tolmachev were executed during Stalin's Great Terror. Eismont was spared this fate by a fatal automobile accident before the Great Terror.

The following excerpt from the stenogram of the Politburo meeting starts with Smirnov's assertion that these accusations were "absolute lies."[4] As the meeting progresses, the desperation of Smirnov grows as he understands the seriousness of his situation and sees the piling on of Stalin's associates. The attack is led by Stalin loyalists—his deputy, Lazar Kaganovich, his trade minister, Anastas Mikoian, and his heavy industry minister, Sergo Ordzhonikidze.

Kaganovich: Here is the declaration of Tolmachev [from his OGPU interrogation]: "Smirnov, as always, railed against the measures of the party leadership, although Eismont did not say anything that was anti-party. . . ."

Smirnov: I declare that this is absolute slander. I assure you. Let them interrogate us. We never met. I repeat a third time: this did not happen.

Kaganovich: Let's return to matters of substance. How was this profanity against the policies of the Central Committee and leadership expressed?

Smirnov: They are absolute lies.

Stalin: Comrade Smirnov. Place yourself in the position of the Central Committee and the Central Control Commission. Comrade Savelev—an old party member, you know that he is an honest person, comes to the Central Committee, and says that Nikolskii, a member of the party, came to him and said this and that, and that he wrote it down. He told Nikolskii that this was a serious business, and that he must inform the Central Committee. In this conversation—his letter relates the conversation between Eismont and Nikolskii—it was said that there is a group which has set as its goal a fundamental change in the party line—that Stalin is confused. But the matter is not only Stalin, of course. The group has as its goal a fundamental change in the party line; they say, that the current party line is leading to the collapse of the country . . . that it is necessary to remove Stalin, displace him or remove him, whatever, that the situation is worsening. This is an anti-party action, this group became particularly agitated after the Northern Caucus events. Comrade Savelev reports to us about this matter and we have no reason to doubt his veracity. He is simply explaining what Nikolskii told him, whose honesty no one can doubt. We checked him out.

Mikoyan: I know him for a long time. He is an honest man who would not lie.

Ordzhonokidze: I also know him.

Stalin: He is not a gossip.

Smirnov: And I am a scoundrel?

Stalin: No, no, wait a minute. Just place yourself in our position. How should we proceed? An honest person—you say that you know him somewhat. I know him a little and not from a bad side. We sent him as an engineer to prepare a road in 1918. He never poked around intelligence circles so that he would fit in—one can't assert that he wanted to benefit himself. And Nikolskii told this honest man about his conversation with Eismont, who was trying to recruit him. Another honest man—Savelev—laid all this out in his letter. Following this, we receive another letter, already certified by Nikolskii, with some amendment to the first letter. What should the Central Committee and Central Control Commission do in this situation?

SMIRNOV: It is clear that they should investigate.

STALIN: Of course. You must know that it is unpleasant for us to move against Foma [Eismont?]. But how should the Central Committee, if it respects itself, and how should the Central Control Commission act when it has two documents from two respected and honest party members. They must investigate. Eismont must be interrogated. His statement is a little confusing but in the main it confirms: Yes, Smirnov and we were very dissatisfied with the policy of the Central Committee; Smirnov complained about the policy of the Central Committee—we already know about this a long time, we received this information from various sources. We know Smirnov; if there is something that he does not like, he will scream and complain about it. But this is a different situation—do they want to change the policy of the Central Committee? It is indeed possible to change the policy, declaring directly—I am a member of the party; you are making a mistake. But they want to change the policy of the Central Committee by creating an illegal group and use words like "remove, replace"—that is, they want something in this fashion. . . . The Central Committee and the Central Control Commission, if they respect themselves, have no choice but to call a meeting and check this out. Now we must check you out. If three confirm the same thing, then you must speak honestly.

SMIRNOV: Let me continue. I am speaking seriously. They were with me only two times; there were other people present. We did not gather and discuss. I again assert this and I am literally trying to prove this. Second. I assert this not only to throw out empty phrases. Comrade Stalin, for me this is not some kind of game. Moreover, one of these comrades I have known since I was a child, even in banishment—Tolmachev. I did not discuss politics with him. I declare one more time that I did not criticize the policy of the party with these comrades, but I spoke in terms of those measures that we should conduct. To give the appearance of criticizing the general party line is incomprehensible to me and to be accused of this is particularly hard on *me.*

STALIN: You can hold to a negative line, but you must tell the Central Committee about this. When you act against the party and gather together people illegally to destroy the party—this is incorrect. Three are speaking out against you. God help you if what you say is correct.

Party Lines, Dictators, and Information

By November of 1932, any person in the Soviet Union holding an official position in the party or state had to be very careful about what he or she said. The Eismont, Tolmachev, and Smirnov case showed that people could not gather privately and express even the slightest reservations about Stalin's policies. They could be overheard. There could be moles in their midst. As Stalin advised, those with doubts should speak directly to Stalin or his Politburo, but that would mean the end of their careers or worse.

It was just such a climate of fear that Stalin, as absolute dictator, wished to create. His few independent and outspoken associates would be initially praised for their candor but would soon find themselves without a job or with a bullet in the back of their heads.

Dictators, however, need to know the truth. If none of their associates are willing to speak out, especially to deliver unpleasant information, the dictator suffers from the curse of poor information. Economic, social, and political systems cannot function without correct information. Policies cannot be improved unless their defects are known and discussed.

Chapter Twelve

Invading Afghanistan

Background

On Christmas Day 1979, U.S. intelligence detected waves of Soviet military aircraft flying into Afghanistan. The next day, President Carter received a memo from his national security advisor outlining possible responses to a wide-scale Soviet intervention.[1] On the night of December 27, Soviet KGB troops dressed in Afghan uniforms attacked the palace where Afghan president Amin was hiding, executed him, and occupied strategic locations throughout Kabul in a forty-five-minute operation. A radio broadcast, purporting to be from Kabul but actually coming from Uzbekistan, announced that Amin's execution had been ordered by the Afghan People's Revolutionary Council and that a new government headed by Soviet-loyalist Babrak Karmal had been formed. Soviet ground forces and paratroopers invaded the same evening, and within five weeks, five divisions were in place. So began the Soviet-Afghanistan war.

The Soviet invasion set off a firestorm of protest and isolated the Soviet state. The 1980 Summer Olympics, which were to showcase Soviet achievements, were overshadowed by an international boycott. During the nine-year war, 620,000 Soviet troops served in Afghanistan. Almost 15,000 were killed and 54,000 wounded. The USSR completed its withdrawal of troops in February of 1989, leaving behind an Afghanistan that would be ravaged by civil war for another decade, with the eventual victory of the Taliban. The Afghanistan war weakened the international prestige of the USSR, brought to life a human rights movement, and filled Soviet cities and towns with disenchanted veterans, many plagued by chronic illnesses or by drug abuse.[2]

This is the story behind the December 1979 invasion decision as told by the official documents of the body that made the decision, the Politburo.[3] The invasion was ordered by a Politburo of aging and ill leaders. Leonid Brezhnev, the party General Secretary, was incapacitated much of 1979. The Brezhnevs, Suslovs, Gromykos, Kosygins, and Andropovs, who were the principal actors in this story, represented Stalin's second generation of party leaders who replaced the first generation of "Old Bolsheviks" he annihilated during the Great Terror. They would not be around to deal with the long-term consequences of their decision, which fell to a third generation of party leaders, headed by Mikhail Gorbachev. Both Brezhnev and party ideologist Mikhail Suslov were to die in 1982. KGB head Yury Andropov, whose intelligence prompted the decision, was already suffering from a fatal kidney disease, and the head of state, Aleksei Kosygin, would pass from the scene in less than a year.

Protecting the April Revolution

After Afghanistan's "April revolution" on April 27, 1978, brought a pro-Soviet government to power, the Democratic Republic of Afghanistan (DRA) turned to its Soviet patrons for assistance in their battle against Muslim insurgents and warlords. The government of Prime Minister Hafizullah Amin and President Nur Mohammad Taraki sought and received Soviet economic assistance and military equipment and advisors but failed to receive ground troops despite repeated requests. The Politburo did not want to fight Afghanistan's battles while its clients sat safe in their fortified offices in Kabul.

On March 18, 1979, the Politburo created a commission comprised of Andrei Gromyko, the foreign minister; Yury Andropov, the head of the KGB; Dmitry Ustinov, minister of defense; and Politburo member Boris Ponomarev, to assess the Afghanistan situation. Their charge came after two panicked requests from President Taraki, on March 18 and 20, for ground troops to put down a mutiny in the town of Herat. Two Soviet advisors had already been killed.

In their conversation with Taraki, Politburo members, led by head of state Kosygin, made it clear that the Afghan government, like the North Vietnamese, should solve their own internal problems:

> The introduction of our troops would arouse the international community, which could lead to a series of negative consequences and would give enemies an excuse to introduce hostile armed formations on Afghan territory.

Instead, the Politburo representatives recommended the Afghans engage in diplomacy "to remove the excuse of Iran, Pakistan and India to meddle in your affairs." Taraki's more modest request—attack helicopters manned by Soviet crews and crews to operate Soviet tanks—was also met with a cool reaction: "The question of sending our people to man your tanks and shoot at your people is a very controversial political issue."

Any remaining hopes for Soviet troops were dashed later in the day by party general secretary Leonid Brezhnev:

> We have examined this matter with extreme care and I can tell you directly: This is not going to be. It would only play into the hands of enemies—both yours and ours. You have already had a more detailed discussion with our comrades, and we hope that you accept with understanding our considerations. Of course, to declare this publicly, either by you or by us, that we are not going to do this [commit troops], for understandable reasons, does not make sense.

After these conversations, Afghan forces quelled the Herat mutiny without Soviet ground troops, and the Politburo commission went about preparing its position paper on Afghanistan. Their report was discussed and its recommendations accepted three weeks later at the April 12, 1979, meeting of the Politburo under the agenda item: "About our future course in Afghanistan."

The eleven-page report came out unequivocally against the use of ground troops. It provided a sober assessment, garbed in Marxist language of class struggle and counter-revolutionary forces. It concluded that the Afghan socialist revolution was in difficulty. It was being applied in a primitive country without a strong working class and was being challenged by religious fanatics, foreign interventionists, tribal warlords, and bourgeois elements. To make matters worse, the Afghan party, divided on tribal lines between the "Khalq" and "Parcham" factions, was in the midst of a power struggle. As the report complained: "The most visible leaders of the Parcham group [including the later president Babrak Karmal] have been either physically eliminated, removed from party work, or driven out of army and state administration; others have fled abroad as political emigrants."

Under these circumstances, Soviet troops should not be committed:

> In view of the primarily internal character of anti-government actions in Afghanistan, the use of our troops in suppressing them would, on the one hand, seriously harm our international integrity and would turn back the process of détente. It would also reveal the weak position of the Taraki government and further encourage counter-revolutionaries inside and outside Afghanistan to step up their anti-government activities.... Our decision not to honor the request of the leaders of the Democratic Republic of Afghanistan to send Soviet troops is completely correct. It is necessary to stick to this line and in the case of new anti-government actions to rule out the possibility of the use of troops.

Certain types of assistance were, however, to be encouraged, such as political and military training, shipments of grain and military equipments, and advice on "strengthening and raising the effectiveness of organs of state security."

Eight months later, the same Politburo that categorically refused to commit ground troops ordered the invasion of Afghanistan from bases in Soviet Turkistan. Eventually more than a half a million troops were to serve in the Afghanistan venture. The mission of these troops changed along the way from installing and protecting a new government, to counter-insurgency operations, and then to air and ground operations.

This story is about what happened to change the Soviet leadership's mind. It tells the tale of how an increasingly paranoid and suspicious gerontocracy accepted the KGB's theory that imperialist forces, headed by the United States, intended to threaten its southernmost republics from Afghanistan as part of a vast conspiracy to create a second Ottoman Empire. The final decision was made at the summer home of the ailing Leonid Brezhnev by a handful of Politburo members that did not include those most likely to raise questions about the forthcoming adventure.

The Dynamics of Afghanistan Policy

There was an eight-month interval between the Politburo's "firm" decision not to commit troops on April 12 and the invasion on the night of December 27 to 28. Initially, the Politburo continued to send out negative signals concerning the use of Soviet troops. The ambassador was instructed to tell the Afghans, who were pressing for Soviet helicopter crews, that "such attack helicopters, operated by Afghan crews, in combination with other air force detachments, can [alone] carry out the mission of suppressing counter-revolutionary actions."

Throughout the eight-month interim, Afghanistan policy was overseen by the same committee of four (Gromyko, Andropov, Ustinov, and Ponomarev) who devised the April 12 strategy. As they monitored events, they saw few signs of encouragement. In a report dated June 28, they complained about the follies and missteps of the increasingly dictatorial Afghan government. Ominously, they recommended that, in addition to senior specialists to advise the Afghan army, special KGB troops (disguised as technicians) be sent in to protect the Soviet embassy along with a detachment of paratroopers (disguised as maintenance personnel) to protect key government facilities. Presumably, the disguises were to fool Afghan government officials as the Soviets covertly built up a military presence in the country. Indeed, it was such clandestine forces of the KGB that executed Amin the night of December 27.

We do not have access to the secret reports submitted to the Politburo by KGB and military intelligence during this period, but it was the KGB, under Andropov, that began to detect signs of a vast conspiracy by the United States and its allies. The KGB's growing suspicion was prompted by a bloody coup which removed the general secretary of the Afghan party, Taraki.

In September of 1979, the simmering feud between President (and party general secretary) Taraki and Prime Minister Amin boiled over. Taraki perished in a coup organized by Amin, who was now in sole charge and whose actions increasingly alarmed his watchers in Andropov's KGB. The KGB became increasingly suspicious as Amin sought reconciliation with opposition groups, purged the government of party members, and even made overtures to the American CIA.

The turning point came in early December with Andropov's alarming memo to Brezhnev, in which he warned that Amin's actions were "threatening the achievements of the April revolution." Specifically Andropov wrote that the situation in Afghanistan had taken an "undesirable turn for us," that Amin may be making a "possible political shift to the West," including "contacts with an American agent that are kept secret from us" and promises to tribal leaders to adopt a policy of neutrality.

Andropov offered a solution to Amin's treachery. He had been contacted by exiled Afghan communists, in particular by Babrak Karmal, who had "worked out a plan for opposing Amin and for creating 'new' party and state organs." In other words, Andropov had exiled Afghan communists lined up to take over after a coup to remove Amin. These exiled Afghan compatriots, according to Andropov "have raised the question of possible assistance, in case of need, including military." Clearly the exiles did not have enough support to overthrow Amin on their own.

Andropov went on to note that the current Soviet military presence in Afghanistan was probably sufficient to render such "assistance" but "as a precautionary measure in the event of unforeseen complications, it would be wise to have a military group close to the border." Such military force would allow the Soviets to "decide various questions pertaining to the liquidation of gangs" (presumably the liquidation of Amin).[4]

The Andropov stance became the policy mantra of the Andropov, Gromyko, Ustinov, and Ponomarev commission, which in its subsequent reports emphasized that "foreign intervention and terror against honest and loyal cadres threaten to destroy the benefits of the April revolution." The Politburo commission accepted Andropov's characterization of Afghanistan as a crisis that had to be resolved quickly.

There is a limited paper trail for the time between the Andropov memo in early December and the actual invasion. There was never a written invasion order; there were fears that the soon-to-be-deposed Amin would get wind. The Politburo began to use code words in its own meetings, and its few official documents refer to "A" (for Afghanistan) and "measures" to denote the invasion and the associated coup against Amin.

According to the memoirs of a knowledgeable Soviet military official, a meeting was held in Brezhnev's private office on December 8,[5] attended by Andropov, Gromyko, Suslov and Ustinov, to discuss a possible invasion. Andropov and Ustinov purportedly cited CIA plans to threaten the USSR's southern flank with missiles in Afghanistan, and cited the danger that Afghan uranium deposits could be used by Pakistan and Iraq. At the end of the meeting, two options were identified: (1) to remove Amin by the hands of KGB special agents and replace him with the loyal Babrak Karmal; (2) to accomplish the same by sending in Soviet troops. An invasion was still up in the air, but it was already decided that Amin had to be removed.

On December 10, defense minister and Politburo subcommittee member Ustinov ordered the chief of the general staff, N. V. Ogarkov, to prepare eighty thousand troops for the "measure." The chief of staff purportedly objected, saying that the "measure" could not be carried out with such a number of troops, but was told to obey Politburo orders. On the same day, Ogarkov was summoned to a meeting with Brezhnev and the Politburo subcommittee where he failed to persuade the Politburo not to use force. That evening, Ustinov ordered the military leadership to prepare for the invasion, and troops were mobilized in the staging area in Turkistan.

The actual decision to invade Afghanistan was made at a meeting held in Brezhnev's country house two days later, on December 12. The meeting was attended by four of the fifteen Politburo members (Brezhnev, Ustinov, Gromyko, and Chernenko). Andropov was notably absent [unless the attendance record is inaccurate], but he was well informed about what was going to transpire. The resolution was written by hand by Konstantin Chernenko (to ensure absolute secrecy) and was entitled "About the situation in 'A' [code word for Afghanistan]" and reads:

> 1. Confirm the measures [code word for invasion] proposed by Andropov, Ustinov, and Gromyko, authorizing them to make minor changes in the course of execution of these measures. Questions that require a decision from the Central Committee should be introduced to the Politburo.

Handwritten document with Politburo members' signatures authorizing the Afghan war.

Andropov, Ustinov, and Gromyko are charged with carrying out these measures. 2. Andropov, Ustinov and Gromyko should keep the Politburo informed on the execution of these measures. Signed L. BREZHNEV.

This handwritten decree was placed in a special safe.

The Politburo was comprised of fifteen members, but the decision was made, presumably in the strictest of secrecy, by only six of them, including, of course, party general secretary Brezhnev. It was not until the day before the invasion that the plan to invade was presented to the full Politburo (on December 26). With the "measures" ready to go into operation within twenty-four hours, it was clear that the full Politburo was to act as a rubber stamp. It is noteworthy that the protocols approved at this Politburo meeting continue to use veiled language and code words. After a presentation of the invasion plan by the Afghanistan commission, general secretary Brezhnev spoke in indirect language:

> [Brezhnev] expressed a series of wishes to approve this plan of action, mentioned by these comrades, for the near future. It was recognized as wise for the Commission of the Politburo, given the contents and direction of the reported plan, to carefully weigh each step of its actions. Questions where it would be necessary to obtain decisions should be brought to the Central Committee on a timely basis.

At this meeting, each Politburo member was asked to sign the handwritten decree "About the situation in 'A'" prepared at Brezhnev's dacha on December 12. According to the dates of the signatures scrawled across the page, some had already signed off the day before, but two signed on the day of the presentation (December 26). Notably, there is no signature of Kosygin, the head of state, who was notably absent from the meeting and was a known opponent of the invasion.

Informing the Central Committee

The decision to invade Afghanistan was made by the head of the Communist Party, general secretary Brezhnev, and a four-person subcommittee of the fifteen-member Politburo. The Politburo's job, in theory, was to manage the affairs of the Central Committee comprised of national and regional party leaders. The head of state and Politburo member, Aleksei Kosygin, was notably absent when the final decision was made. The Soviet government, as such, did not participate in the decision. Only after the invasion did state agencies swing into action, such as negotiating the terms of the treaty for stationing troops, or the foreign ministry's presentation of the Soviet case to foreign governments and to the United Nations.

That the decision was made by Brezhnev and his Politburo colleagues is not surprising. Article Six of the 1977 USSR Constitution states that "the leading and guiding force of the Soviet society and the nucleus of its political system, of all state and public organizations, is the Communist Party of the Soviet Union. The Communist Party, armed with Marxism-Leninism, determines the general perspectives of the development of society and the course of the home and foreign policy of the USSR, directs the great constructive work of the Soviet people, and imparts a planned, systematic and theoretically substantiated character to their struggle for the victory of communism."[6]

The constitution does not define how or who in the Communist Party makes decisions about war and peace, but, since the days of Lenin, they were to be made by the Politburo.

The Central Committee was officially informed (briefed) by the Politburo subcommittee four days after the invasion had taken place (December 31) in a report entitled "About the events in Afghanistan on December 27–28." The Politburo had instructed its Afghanistan committee to bring decisions to the Central Committee "on a timely basis." In this case, "timely" meant after the fact. The Politburo report notably did not ask the Central Committee for approval of its actions; it was simply a briefing memorandum designed to give Central Committee members appropriate talking points.

The talking points were that the Amin government had brought Afghanistan to a state of crisis. It had removed those who had created the April revolution ("murdering six hundred party members without court approval"). The Amin government had turned to a "more balanced foreign policy," which included confidential meetings with American agents. The Amin government had tried "to simplify its position by compromising with the leaders of internal counter-revolutionary forces," including leaders of the "extreme Muslim op-position." A key talking point was that a reluctant Soviet Union had been invited by an opposition that had united against Amin to "save the fatherland and the revolution" and had complied by sending a "limited contingent of troops." These troops would withdraw once the April revolution had been saved. In fact, "the wide public masses of Afghanistan welcomed the overthrow of the Amin regime with un-concealed joy and are prepared to support the declared program of the new government."

The Battle for World Opinion

The Politburo faced an uphill public relations battle after the inva-sion. Its official story was full of holes. Its troops and special forces had somehow been invited to assist the Afghanistan revolution by puppet leaders appointed only after the coup. Amin was supposedly condemned to death by a fictitious Afghanistan Revolutionary Coun-cil. Radio announcements of these events had originated from within the Soviet Union, not from Kabul.

The Soviet propaganda machine sprang into full gear. The major talking points were distributed to forty-six "communist and workers parties of non-socialist parties" in a memo entitled "About the propa-gandistic coverage of our actions in relation to Afghanistan." These friendly communist and socialist parties were given six points:

1. The Soviet Union sent troops at the request of the Afghanistan leadership.
2. The Afghanistan government requested Soviet assistance only for their battle against foreign aggression.
3. Foreign aggression threatens the Afghan revolution and its sovereignty and independence.
4. The request for assistance came from a sovereign Afghan government to another sovereign Soviet government.
5. The naming of the new leadership of Afghanistan was an internal matter decided by its own Revolutionary Council.
6. The Soviet Union had nothing to do with the change in government, which was exclusively an internal matter.

Although some of these points defied credibility, they were neverthe-less supplied for the public discourse.

An even more urgent need was to coach the new Afghan govern-ment on how to conduct diplomacy. Already on January 4, 1980, the wily Andrei Gromyko, long the face of Soviet diplomacy, instructed the new Afghan foreign minister (Dost) on how to present the case to the Security Council of the United Nations. The "Memo of the basic points of a conversation of Gromyko with foreign minister Dost. Janu-ary 4, 1980" comprises a monolog by Gromyko, rather than a "conver-sation" between him and Dost.

GROMYKO: I want to share with you, Comrade Minister, some thoughts about the U.N. Security Council and your forthcoming remarks. Of course, these ideas are not final, but they reflect the views of our country about the events in Afghanistan and its vicinity. First. Western powers, particularly the United States, have launched hostile propaganda against the Soviet Union and against revolutionary Afghanistan. Imperialism has decided to "blow off steam." Second. With respect to the tone of your presentation at the Security Council, you should not act as the accused but as the accuser. I think there are enough facts for this position. Therefore it is extremely important not to defend but to attack. Third. It is essential to emphasize that the introduction of the limited military contingent in Afghanistan was done by the Soviet Union in response to numerous requests of the government of Afghanistan. These requests were made earlier by Taraki when he was in Moscow and by Amin. Carter wants to create the impression that the Soviet Union received this request only from the new government of Afghanistan, but you can decisively refute this notion using exact dates and details. Fourth. You must clearly emphasize that the limited Soviet contingent was introduced to Afghanistan only to assist against unceasingly aggressive forces, particularly from Pakistan, where refugee camps have been converted by the forces of the United States, other Western countries, and China into staging areas for foreign fighters. Fifth. The change of leadership in Afghanistan is a purely internal matter. No one has the right to tell Afghanistan what to do or how to act.

Dost's role in this conversation was to listen and then to thank Gromyko for his time and remarks.

Gorbachev: Pulling Out of Afghanistan

Mikhail Gorbachev became general secretary of the Communist Party in March of 1985. He inherited a war that had become a Vietnam-like quagmire. From its earliest days of power, the Gorbachev team, led by foreign minister Eduard Shevardnadze, concluded that the Soviet Union must find a face-saving way out of Afghanistan. The ineffective Babrak Karmal was replaced by the former chief of the Afghan secret police, Mohammad Najibullah, who also was unable to negotiate a national reconciliation. In 1988, the governments of Afghanistan and Pakistan signed an agreement known as the Geneva Accords, which called for the withdrawal of Soviet troops with a United Nations' special mission to oversee the agreement. On February 15, 1989, the last Soviet troops were withdrawn, but the civil war continued and, in fact, never ended. By 1996, the Taliban had gained control of most of Afghanistan, although hostilities continued, and they ruled from 1996 until their ouster in 2001.

The Soviet withdrawal represented one of the low points in Soviet history. One of the last documents in the Central Committee files is a position paper prepared by Shevardnadze and five other Politburo members on January 23, 1989, three weeks before the departure of the last contingent of Soviet troops. The downbeat memo confirms the tense situation in Afghanistan as both sides awaited the February 15 deadline:

> The government is holding its positions but only due to the assistance of Soviet troops and all understand that the main battle lies ahead. The opposition has even reduced its activities, saving its strength for the next period. Comrade Najibullah thinks that they are prepared to move after the withdrawal. Our Afghan comrades are seriously concerned as to what will happen. . . . They express their understanding of the decision to withdraw troops but soberly think they cannot manage without our troops.
>
> The current situation raises for us a number of complicated issues. On the one hand, if we renege on our decision to withdraw troops by

February 15, there would be extremely undesirable complications on the international front. On the other hand, there is no certainty that after our withdrawal there will not be an extremely serious threat to a regime which the entire world associates with us. Moreover, the opposition can at any time begin to coordinate its activities, which is what American and Pakistan military circles are pushing for. There is a also a danger that there is no true unity in the Afghanistan party, which is split into factions and clans.

The memo concludes that the Afghan government can hold Kabul and other cities, but expresses concern that a siege could starve out these cities. Soviet troops would be needed to keep supply lines open, but there is no way, under existing agreements, to keep them in the country.

In effect, the Gorbachev government was conceding that Afghanistan was lost and that there was nothing the Soviet Union could do to stop it. The USSR's reputation would be damaged and its influence in the region lost. Gorbachev's decision not to further prop up foreign communist regimes became the Gorbachev Doctrine of non-intervention in Eastern Europe and East Germany.

Lessons of Afghanistan

The war in Afghanistan was the USSR's "Vietnam." It de-legitimized the authority of the Communist Party. The mighty Soviet army, the victor against Hitler in World War II, was dealt a humiliating defeat. Soviet society was filled with more than a half million disenchanted Afghan veterans, many wounded, sick, drug addicted, and forming into criminal gangs. The vaunted Soviet army showed itself totally unprepared for guerilla warfare. The Afghan war gave rise to the first serious dissident movement within Russia. In the longer run, the Soviet battle against Islamic forces promoted Islamic fundamentalism in Central Asia and in Chechnya.

Countries go to war in different ways. Although the U.S. entry into Vietnam was without a congressional declaration of war, there was widespread debate within government circles, the press, and within society before, during, and after the war. The first and second Gulf wars against Saddam Hussein were also the subject of public debate and discourse both in Congress and in the United Nations. There was dissent and disagreement (war opponents would argue there was too little debate), but there was a public forum for public debate.

A remarkable feature of the Soviet invasion of Afghanistan is that it was made by so few people with so little input from government, press, or society. Official Soviet policy, which was devised by a few Politburo members, was initially against any invasion at that time or in the future. The negative consequences were clearly understood and spelled out. Yet within the course of a few months, the same individuals changed their minds, largely due to the influence of a few Politburo members (the foreign minister, the KGB head, and the defense minister) and based on the notion of an imminent offensive challenge from the United States that did not exist.

The American decision to invade Iraq was based in part on intelligence that Saddam Hussein had massive stockpiles of weapons of mass destruction. The Soviet decision to invade Afghanistan was based on the KGB's faulty intelligence that the United States had a master plan to use Afghanistan to threaten Soviet republics in Central Asia. Similarly, the U.S. intelligence community viewed the Soviet Afghan invasion as a master plan to fulfill "the age-long dream of Moscow to have direct access to the Indian Ocean" and to drive "right down on the edge of the Arabian and Oman Gulfs."[7] Both thought they were playing defense to the other's offense.

The American Vietnam experience has shown that those who order ill-fated wars pay the political consequences, such as Lyndon Johnson or Richard Nixon in Vietnam. Soviet experience shows that there were no consequences of bad decision making. Yury Andropov, the head of the KGB, was more responsible than any other Soviet official for the Afghanistan invasion, which was clearly evident as a disastrous miscalculation by 1982. Yet, upon the death of Leonid Brezhnev on November 12, 1982, he was elected to the highest position—party general secretary—on the same day.

The Politburo of Leonid Brezhnev made another fundamental mistake. Although its reports mention Islamic fundamentalism, it continued to regard the United States, China, and the government of Pakistan as those controlling the levers of the conflict. Viewing the world through the prism of Marxist thought, there was no room in their vision for a Taliban, a Mullah Omar, or an Osama bin Laden. The absence of this insight came back to haunt post-Brezhnev and post-Gorbachev Russia in Chechnya and in the growing restiveness of the Muslim populations of Central Asia. A similar U.S. miscalculation ended on September 11, 2001.

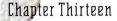

Chapter Thirteen

"Arbeit Macht Frei"[1] Soviet Style

Background

Throughout most of Stalin's reign, the functions of state security were combined in one massive organization called the NKVD. After the war, there was a separation of security functions between the Ministry of Internal Affairs (MVD) and what would eventually become the Committee for State Security, the KGB. After Stalin's death, this separation continued. The MVD was headed by S. N. Kruglov, a veteran state-security official, who replaced Lavrenty Beria upon his arrest in the summer of 1953. Ivan Serov headed the KGB, which was charged with domestic and foreign intelligence and operations.

Stalin's successors were left with the problem of what to do with the Gulag camps and their two and a half million inmates. Within weeks of Stalin's death, more than a million inmates were amnestied, primarily those who had committed minor offenses. But more than a million political inmates, nationalists, and hardened criminals were left in camps. Many of them erupted into violent revolts in the wake of the first amnesty.

The amnesty of political prisoners had to await Nikita Khrushchev's February 1956 secret speech, which revealed the horrors of the Stalin regime. Khrushchev's speech signaled that it was now time to decide what to do with the Gulag camps and their inhabitants. He turned to his two state-security agencies for proposals. The MVD proposed to replace the Gulag camps with conventional prisons and to eliminate the use of forced labor as a major input into the economy. The KGB argued in favor of keeping as much of Stalin's Gulag as possible and argued with particular fervor for the continuation of forced convict labor.

This is the story of the battle between the "moderate" Ministry of Internal Affairs, headed by Kruglov, and the "hardliner" KGB headed by Ivan Serov. Of the two, Kruglov had more experience. He headed the Gulag from 1946 to 1953. The moderate–"hardliner" battle is captured in a document from Ivan Serov to the Central Committee (addressed to Leonid Brezhnev).[2] According to Serov, forced labor was actually good for prisoners—a Soviet form of "Arbeit macht frei."

The KGB's Argument

In a memo of May 10, 1956, KGB head Serov strongly resisted his rival MVD's proposal to liquidate the corrective-labor camps and to transfer the inmates of the Gulag to prisons on two grounds:

> First, inmates in prisons cannot be used for socially necessary labor because there are no enterprises in prisons. Accordingly, there can be no use of the factor most important to re-educating the prisoner—his labor.

> Second, the liquidation of the corrective labor camps requires an expansion of prisons for holding non-working prisoners at additional expense of state resources.

According to Serov's calculations, there were already 152,000 inmates in prisons built to house 104,000. If the Gulag camps were emptied, the prisons would have to accommodate an additional 113,000 counter-revolutionaries, 135,000 thieves, bandits and murderers, and 305,000 criminals convicted of large thefts, for a total of over 554,000. This would yield a figure six times greater than the existing capacity of prisons.

Serov also objected to the MVD's proposal to prohibit the use of prison labor in construction, forestry, mining, and other hard physical labor.

The use of prisoners for socially necessary labor including heavy labor, if correctly organized with adequate supplies and in the context of educational work, will aid the re-education of workers in the spirit of an honest life of labor in Soviet society. Moreover, practice shows that, if well organized, such work can raise the worker's qualifications.

The KGB also opposed the MVD's proposal to create special prisons for unredeemable criminals:

The concentration of so-called unredeemable criminals in one place can create the view among them of hopelessness for the future. It is not ruled out that in such prisons there will be organized demonstrations, rebellions and other excesses instead of work.

The KGB also opposed the MVD's proposal to relax the conditions of incarceration for prisoners showing positive signs of rehabilitation, such as giving them the right to live outside the prison or with their families.

The introduction of such a regime will weaken the entire regime of holding prisoners and the re-educational meaning of prison confinement will be lost. If prisoners have served a major portion of their time and are showing a positive attitude toward work, then it is necessary to consider their early release.

Kruglov and his MVD, as experienced Gulag operators, understood the power of the so-called work credit system. Work credits were granted to prisoners who over-fulfilled their plans. For each work credit received the sentence would be shortened according to an existing formula. Although work credits were periodically banned in the Gulag, they kept being revived because of their effectiveness in stimulating work effort.

Serov and his KGB opposed the continuation of work credits. Instead, they proposed to leave early releases to the courts and to prison managers. An automatic system of early releases could unleash undesirable elements on civil society.

The current practice of awarding work credits for the over-fulfillment of plans leads to the result that inmates possessing good work habits and physical strength have the opportunity to obtain early release, without showing signs of rehabilitation. Such early-released persons cause concern among citizens and in addition they tend to commit new crimes. It would be better, in exceptional circumstances, when an inmate with exceptional labor service and behavior earns the right to early release after having served the major part of his sentence, to let courts decide based upon a proposal of the camp director.

Who Won?

The issue of the future of the Russian penal system was joined after Stalin's death, with two visions presented. One called for a conventional prison system focused on rehabilitation; the other (KGB) position proposed the continuation of a forced labor system in camps with strict terms of confinement. In the long run, both positions partially won the day. Russia today has a penal system that is a mix of Stalinist and Western practices.

Prisons remained under the jurisdiction of the MVD (now the MVD of the Russian Federation) until 1996, when they were transferred to local authorities. The Gulag system of camp administration was officially abolished in 1965, although prisoners continued to be assigned to work with hazardous chemicals and in timber cutting. Modern Russian penal legislation resembles that of Western countries, with prohibition of torture and inhumane practices. Russian prisons and camps remain overcrowded, with some 20 percent of the prison population incarcerated in detention centers due to lack of space. More than half of Russian prisoners are held today in overcrowded labor camps, where they work primarily in logging operations.[3]

The most striking legacy of this debate is the exceptionally high percentage of the Russian population institutionalized in prisons and camps. In 1970, there were slightly more than a million convicts. There were also innovations in the late Soviet period such as "punitive psychiatry," which made political activities such as dissidence a mental illness, requiring confinement in mental hospitals. From that day on, political prisoners ended up in hospitals not in prisons. By the mid-1980s, the prison population doubled to more than 2 million.

During the disorder of Gorbachev's *perestroika,* the decline in convictions outweighed the increase in crime and reduced the number of prisoners back to 1.3 million by 1991. The Russian institutionalized population at the turn of the twenty-first century remained high by international standards (along with the United States) at one million, or 632 per hundred thousand, versus the world average of 86 prisoners per hundred thousand.[4]

Chapter Fourteen

Vladimir Moroz

Stalin's Orphans

Background

Vladimir Moroz was born in 1922, the son of a mid-level party official in Moscow. Vladimir had an older and a younger brother. On November 2, 1937, his father was arrested and executed for anti-Soviet activity. His mother was sentenced to five years in the Gulag as a traitor to the fatherland. His older brother was sentenced to five years for belonging to an anti-Soviet youth organization. Vladimir, then fifteen, and his nine-year-old brother were sent to separate NKVD orphanages. Vladimir, although he was less than sixteen at the time, was sentenced to prison for anti-Soviet statements made in the orphanage and in letters, and, according to registration statistics, died at the age of seventeen in Prison No. 1 in the city of Kuznetsk on April 28, 1939. Vladimir and his family were posthumously rehabilitated in 1956 as a result of petitions by his older brother, who survived the Great Terror.

This is the story of Vladimir Moroz as told largely by his case file from the archives of the NKVD.[1]

The Case Against Vladimir Moroz

According to NKVD records, Vladimir was not an ideal student in his NKVD orphanage in Annenkovo: "He expressed dissatisfaction with the arrests of his family by the NKVD in conversations and letters." Excerpts from his interrogation by an NKVD sergeant on April 24, 1938, reveal his "confession":

NKVD: Our investigation shows that during your stay in the Annenkovo orphanage you conducted counter-revolutionary activity. Tell us about the details.

Moroz: I did not conduct any counter-revolutionary activity.

NKVD: You are lying. The investigation requires a complete confession.

Moroz: I repeat that I did not conduct counter-revolutionary activity.

NKVD: We found your letter of counter-revolutionary content. What do you have to say about this?

[At this point in the interrogation, Moroz's tone changes to one of submission. We would guess that he was tortured at this point. His confession then uses standard NKVD language, which is underlined in the text. These parts of the confession may have been drafted by the interrogator for his signature.]

Moroz: Yes, these letters have counter-revolutionary content and I am the author. In these letters I expressed evident hostility to Soviet construction, praising Trotsky-Bukharin bandits while sympathizing with the condemned and executed enemies of the people, and I compromised the leaders of the party and Soviet state and personally Stalin.

The NKVD's conclusion of June 14, 1938: The fifteen-year-old Moroz had violated Article 58 of the Russian criminal codex (counter-revolution) by "defaming the leaders of the party and Soviet state and personally Stalin." Vladimir was sentenced by a special NKVD tribunal to three years in a corrective-labor camp on October 25, 1938. He survived there less than half a year.

Moroz's Letter to Stalin

On November 18, 1938, Vladimir wrote a letter to Stalin asking his assistance. The letter was apparently still written from the orphanage.

He had not yet been transferred to the prison, and he probably did not know of his sentence to the Gulag because he complains largely about conditions in the school:

> Respected Comrade Stalin!
>
> I am obliged to turn to you for assistance. It is necessary because of my unbearable situation. I read in the paper about your answer to Comrade Ivanov and I hoped that you would answer me as well. What is unbearable about my current situation? My Father, G. S. Moroz, was arrested by the NKVD after which followed the arrest of my Mother for unknown reasons. I endured blow after blow, misfortune after misfortune. They sent me to the village of Annenkovo. You can imagine my situation in the orphanage. I have dark thoughts; I have become a misanthrope: I have isolated myself from others, in every face I see a hidden enemy, I have lost faith in people.

The letter then reveals why Vladimir was singled out for punishment: As an intelligent and privileged son of a party official, he writes that his school is wretched and that he knows more than his teachers. With such an attitude, his NKVD handlers in the orphanage would have singled him out:

> Why am I alone? Only because the general intellectual level of the teachers is lower than my own. This is not self praise. The school is so wretched, the teachers so mediocre, that there is no wish to attend classes. I want to receive the maximum knowledge but here you receive less than the minimum. How can one be satisfied with that? You may think that I am too coddled, sentimental. No, this is not the case. I only demand happiness, current happiness, happiness that is enduring.

Vladimir's letter ends:

> Comrade Stalin: I am sinking faster and faster into some kind of bottomless pit, from which there is no escape. Save me. Help me. Don't let me perish! This is all I have to say. I hope that you will answer me soon and help me. I am awaiting with impatience your reply.

Of course, there was no response from Stalin.

Photographic portrait of the "Great and Generous Leader," Joseph Stalin.

A Mother's Plea for an Already-Dead Son

Vladimir died in prison on April 28, 1939. His mother, serving her Gulag sentence, was unaware of the fate of her husband (already executed) and three sons (the eldest in prison, the two younger at least initially in NKVD orphanages). She wrote to NKVD head Lavrenty Beria on September 9, 1939, half a year after Vladimir's death, the following plea:

> In the camp, I asked about the fate of my sons and it was communicated to me in March of 1938 that two sons, the fifteen-year-old Vladimir and the nine-year-old Aleksandr, are in the orphanage in Annenkovo in the Kuznetsk region. They did not tell me anything about my eldest son, Samuil. I turned many times to the Moscow NKVD with requests to tell me about my eldest son. Finally, at the end of May 1939, the Moscow NKVD told me that both Samuil and Vladimir had been arrested. They did not say when and for what reason. It is also unclear why a youth, who is held in Kuibyshev province in an orphanage, has been arrested by the NKVD of Moscow.
>
> My eldest son finished the tenth grade.
>
> My second son, Vladimir, a student of the eighth grade, received the highest marks and was a young pioneer, with exemplary behavior.
>
> All this information speaks to the fact that they could not have committed crimes independently that would have been subject to arrest by the NKVD. I presume that my sons, like me, were subject to repression as members of the family. But taking into consideration the directives of the party and of Stalin personally—children in no circumstances should answer for the sins of the father—this directive of the Leader, pronounced on several occasions, gives me the right of a mother to direct to you, Citizen Commissar, a petition—to demand an examination by the Moscow NKVD into the charges against my sons.

Rehabilitation

Vladimir Moroz's posthumous rehabilitation was petitioned by his older brother Samuil, who survived Stalin's Great Terror. There is no record in the file of the fates of his mother and younger brother.

On February 8, 1957, the Deputy USSR Prosecutor filed a protest with the Military Collegium of the Supreme Court "About the case of V. G. Moroz." The protest lays out the facts of the execution of Vladimir's father and the arrests of other family members. The protest concedes that Vladimir Moroz indeed made anti-Soviet statements, such as those covered in Article 58, but they were prompted by the "unjustified" persecution of his family members. Moreover, he had not reached the obligatory age of sixteen at the time of sentencing. For these reasons, the prosecutor requested "the decree of the Special Assembly of the NKVD of October 28, 1938, relating to Vladimir Moroz be rescinded and the case be closed because of the absence of a committed crime."

The rehabilitation did not raise Vladimir Moroz from the grave, but it must have given some minor satisfaction to his brother and other survivors to have the charge "enemy of the Soviet people" removed from his brother's name.

Whom Did Stalin Destroy?

The Moroz family was headed by a dedicated communist, a high-ranking party official of the trade ministry. His family enjoyed privileges, living in the regime city of Moscow, probably receiving the famed "Kremlin ration" of food and other goods. Their middle son of fifteen, Vladimir, was a talented student, receiving the highest marks, a young pioneer, and a dedicated communist. It was young people like Vladimir Moroz who carried the promise of Soviet communism.

Vladimir's confiscated diary, written from a bleak NKVD orphanage in the Russian provinces, shows the devastating effect of the Great Terror on him and others like him. He wrote the following words, never realizing that they would show up in print seventy-five years later:

> A person awaking from a lethargic twelve-year dream would be simply stunned by the changes that have taken place. He would not find the old leadership. He would see in the leadership clean-shaven ignoramuses, doing nothing for the victory of the revolution, or elderly do-nothings selling their comrades for their personal gain. He would not see the "former" legendary leaders of the Red Army. He would not see the builders and organizers of the revolution. He would not see talented writers, journal-

ists, engineers, artists, directors, diplomats, and political figures. . . . It is staggering. A clique of gorged, fat people brashly rule and ninety percent of the people are unhappy. . . . Under the pretense of progress, morality is collapsing.

Vladimir was a representative victim of Stalin's purge of the party. Stalin believed that if he was dissatisfied with the current elite, he could destroy it and put a new and improved elite in its place. What happened in fact was that the new elite was made up of the compromisers, do-nothings, lackeys, and non-independent thinkers, who were to lead the Soviet Union and its empire after Stalin's death.

Lost forever were the Vladimir Morozes—the bright, outspoken true believers, under whose guidance the Soviet Union may have taken a quite different path.

notes

[A list of abbreviations of Russian archival sources appears on page 154.]

CHAPTER ONE: "Scurrilous Provocation"

1. Archives of the Soviet Communist Party and Soviet State: microfilm, 1993–2002. RGANI, f. 89 (The Communist Party on Trial), op. 14, d. 1–20 (Hoover Institution Archives).
2. GARF, f. R-9401, op. 2, d. 65, published in *Istoriia Stalinskogo Gulaga,* Vol. 1, Document 169. Report of L. P. Beria to I. V. Stalin and V. M. Molotov "About the course of operations for the deportation of Crimean Tartars," May 19–20, 1944. Top secret.
3. Note that this is the first reference to such a joint commission in the Politburo file.

CHAPTER TWO: The Four Faces of Stalin

1. Boris Bazhanov (translated with commentary by David Doyle), *Bazhanov and the Damnation of Stalin* (Columbus: Ohio State Press, 1990), pp. 104–106.
2. Lars Lih, Oleg Naumov, and Oleg Khlevniuk, editors, *Stalin's Letters to Molotov, 1925–1936.* Letter No. 86 (New Haven: Yale University Press, 1995), p. 239.
3. RGASPI, f. 78, op. 1, d. 455, published in O. V. Khlevniuk, A. V. Kvashonkin, L. P. Kosheleva, and L. A. Rogovaia, *Stalinskoe Politbiuro v 30-e gody: Sbornik dokumentov* (Moskva: AIRO-XX, 1995), pp. 129, 142.
4. RGASPI, f. 558, op. 11, d. 58, p. 80, published in *Istoriia Stalinskogo Gulaga,* Vol. 2, p. 154.
5. RGASPI, f. 558, op. 11, d. 58, p. 77, published in *Istoriia Stalinskogo Gulaga,* Vol. 2, p. 153.
6. RGASPI, f. 558, op. 11, d. 58, p. 80, published in *Istoriia Stalinskogo Gulaga,* Vol. 2, p. 154.
7. RGASPI, f. 17, op. 2, d. 634, pp. 65–135, published in Khlevniuk et al. *Stalinskoe Politbiuro,* cited in O. V. Khlevniuk, *Politbiuro: Mekhanizmy politicheskoi vlasti v 1930-e gody* (Moskva: Rosspen, 1996), pp 216–29.
8. RGASPI, f. 558, op. 11, d. 95, p. 132, cited in O. V. Khlevniuk, R. Davies, L. P. Kosheleva, E. A. Ris, and L. A. Rogovaia, *Stalin i Kaganovich. Perepiska, 1931–1936 gg.* (Moskva: Rosspen, 2001), p. 683.
9. Archives of the Soviet Communist Party, RGANI, f. 89, op. 48, d. 2, p. 1 (Hoover Institution Archives).

10. Archives of the Soviet Communist Party, RGANI, f. 89, op. 48, d. 9, 12, 17, 3; op. 73, d. 121 (Hoover Institution Archives).

11. Lars T. Lih, Oleg V. Naumov, and Oleg V. Khlevniuk, editors, *Stalin's Letters to Molotov* (New Haven: Yale University Press, 1995), p. 50, cited in Paul Gregory, *The Political Economy of Stalinism* (New York: Cambridge, 2004), p. 14.

12. Marc Jansen and Nikita Petrov, *Stalin's Loyal Executioner* (Stanford: Hoover Press, 2002), p. 20.

CHAPTER THREE: Lenin's Brain

1. Archives of the Soviet Communist Party, RGASPI, f. 89 (The Communist Party on Trial), op. 72, d. 2–12 (Hoover Institution Archives).

2. Tilman Spengler, (translated by Shaun Whiteside), *Lenin's Brain* (New York: Farrar, Straus & Giroux, 1993).

3. www.marxists.org/archive/trotsky/works/1925/lenin/12.htm

CHAPTER FOUR: Marginals and Former People

1. N. I. Bukharin. *Izbranye proizvedeniia* (Moskva, 1990), p. 198 . cited in O. I. Cherdakov, *Formirovanie pravookhranitel'noi sistemy sovetskogo gosudarstva v 1917–1936 gg* (Saratov: Izdatel'stvo Saratovskogo universiteta, 2001), p. 57.

2. APRF, f. 3, op. 58, d. 174, pp 42–49 published in V. N. Khaustov, V. P. Naumov, and N. S. Plotnikova, editors, *Lubianka: Stalin i VChK-GPU-OGPU-NKVD. Ianvar' 1922-dekabr', 1936* (Moskva: Mezhdunarodnyi Fond Demokratiia, 2003), pp. 613–616. "Report of L. M. Zakovskii to G. G. Iagoda About Former People," February 16, 1935.

3. David Shearer, *Policing Stalin's Society* (forthcoming).

4. David Shearer, "Social Disorder, Mass Repression, and the NKVD During the 1930s," *Cahiers du Monde russe,* 42/2, 3–4 (April-December), 2001, pp. 519–20.

5. GARF, f. R-9401, op. 12, d. 137, pp. 202–204, published in *Istoriia Stalinskogo Gulaga,* Vol. 1, document No. 23, pp. 156–158.

6. GARF, f. R-7523, op. 89, d. 4408, pp. 18–19, published in *Istoriia Stalinskogo Gulaga,* Vol. 1, Document No. 226, pp. 613–615 (Statistical Appendix). Statistical Data of the Department of Justice Statistics of the Supreme Court of the USSR on the Number of Sentenced in the USSR for the Period 1937 to the First Half of 1955 (excluding those sentenced by special courts).

7. This case is found at the http://www.memorial.run site under the heading "Dva Lenskikh rasstrela."

8. Archives of the Soviet Communist Party, GARF, f. R-9479, op. 1, d. 19, p. 9 (Hoover Institution Archives), published in *Istoriia Stalinskogo Gulaga,* Vol. 1, Document No. 22. Copy. Report of the Deputy Chief of the GULAG Administration I. I. Pliner to the Deputy Chairman of the OGPU G. G. Iagoda About the Purge of Moscow and Leningrad of "Socially Harmful Elements," July 28, 1933.

CHAPTER FIVE: The Great Terror

1. http://www.writing.upenn.edu/~afilreis/Holocaust/wansee-transcript.html
2. Marc Jansen and Nikita Petrov, *Stalin's Loyal Executioner: People's Commissar Nikolai Ezhov* (Stanford: Hoover Press, 2002), p. 189.
3. TsAFSB, f. 66, op. 5, d. 2, pp. 155–174, published in *Istoriia Stalinskogo Gulaga,* Vol. 1, Document No. 58, pp. 268–275.
4. The classic study of the Great Terror remains Robert Conquest's *The Great Terror: A Reassessment* (London: Oxford University Press, 1968).
5. Golfo Alexopoulos, *Stalin's Outcasts: Aliens, Citizens, and the Soviet State, 1926–1936.* (Ithaca: Cornell University Press, 2003), p. 166.
6. Mark Iunge and Rol'f Binner, *"Kak terror stal 'bol'shim'"* (Moscow: AIRO-XX, 2003), pp. 156–163.
7. RGASPI, f. 558, op. 11, d. 1120, pp. 28–44, 48–57, published in V. N. Khaustov, V. P. Naumov, and N. S. Plotnikova, editors, *Lubianka: Stalin i glavnoe upravlenie gosbezopasnosti NKVD 1937–1938* (Moskva: Mezhdunarodnyi Fond Demokratiia, 2004), p. 207.
8. APRF, f. 3, op. 74, d. 21, p. l.
9. APRF, f. 3, op. 58, d. 212, p. 55–78. Memo of M. P. Frinovskii to the Politburo, with attached NKVD Directive No. 00447, published in Khaustov et al., *Lubianka, Stalin i glavnoe upravlenie gosbezopasnosti,* p. 273.
10. TsAFSB, f. 66, op. 5, d. 2, pp. 155–174, published in *Istoriia Stalinskogo Gulaga,* Vol. 1, Document No. 58, pp. 268–9.
11. The ending date is from section III.1 of NKVD Order No. 00447.
12. TsAFSB, f. 66, op. 5, d. 2, pp. 155–174, published in *Istoriia Stalinskogo Gulaga,* Vol. 1, Document No. 58, p. 269.
13. TsAFSB, f. 66, op. 5, d. 2, pp. 155–174, published in *Istoriia Stalinskogo Gulaga,* Vol. 1, Document No. 58, pp. 269–70.
14. TsAFSB, f. 66, op. 5, d. 2, pp. 155–174, published in *Istoriia Stalinskogo Gulaga,* Vol. 1, Document No. 58, pp. 270–2.
15. TsAFSB, f. 66, op. 1, d. 1, p. 42 published in *Istoriia Stalinskogo Gulaga* (Moskva: Rosspen, 2004), Vol. 2, Document No.1, p. 523. Decree of the VChK [Cheka] "About Red Terror." September 2, 1918.
16. TsAFSB, f. 66, op. 5, d. 2, pp. 155–174, published in *Istoriia Stalinskogo Gulaga,* Vol. 1, Document No. 58, p. 272.
17. *Istoriia Stalinskogo Gulaga,* Vol. 1, Document No. 60, pp. 277–280. Operational Order of the NKVD No. 00486 "About the repression of wives and the placement of children of convicted traitors of the motherland," August 15, 1937.
18. GARF, f. R-8131, op. 37, file 145, pp. 193–197, published in *Istoriia Stalinskogo Gulaga,* Vol. 1, Document No. 98, p. 363–365. Declaration of former party workers of Chita province to Deriagin, Secretary of the Chita VKP(b) Committee, about the fabrication of cases by officials of the Chita NKVD Directorate, November 21, 1939.

19. TsAFSB, f. 66, op. 5, d. 2, pp. 155–174, published in *Istoriia Stalinskogo Gulaga,* Vol. 1, Document No. 58, pp. 272–3.

20. This case is found at the http://www.memorial.run site under the heading "Dva Lenskikh rasstrela."

21. APRF, f. 3, op. 24, d. 302, pp. 96–124, published in Khaustov et al., *Lubianka: Stalin i glavnoe upravlenie gosbezopasnosti,* Document No. 60, pp. 144–156. Special Communication of N. I. Ezhov to I. V. Stalin, with attached interrogation of A. S. Enukidze, 28 April 1937.

22. A. Iu. Vatlin, *Terror raionnogo masshtaba: Massovye operatsii NKVD v Kuntsevskom raione Moskovskoi oblasti, 1937–1938gg* (Moskva: Rosspen, 2004), pp. 45, 48.

23. TsAFSB, f. 66, op. 5, d. 2, pp. 155–174 published in *Istoriia Stalinskogo Gulaga,* Vol. 1, Document No. 58, pp. 273–4.

24. APRF, f. 3, op. 58, d. 3, p. 113 (both sides), published in V. N. Khaustov, V. P Naumov, and N. S. Plotnikova, compilers, *Lubianka: Stalin i VChK-GPU-OGPU-NKVD. Ianvar' 1922–dekabr' 1936* (Moskva: Mezhdunarodnyi Fond Demokratiia, 2003), pp. 137–8.

25. Iunge and Binner, p. 226.

26. Iunge and Binner, p. 39.

27. Iunge and Binner, p. 241.

28. TsAFSB, f. 66, op. 5, d. 2, pp. 155–174, published in *Istoriia Stalinskogo Gulaga,* Vol. 1, Document No. 58, p. 274.

29. GARF, f. 9401, op. 8, d. 51, pp. 1–10, published in *Istoriia Stalinskogo Gulaga,* Vol. 2, Document No. 84, p. 173.

30. R. Medvedev and Zh. Medvedev, *Neizvestni Stalin* (Moscow: Folio, 2001), pp. 149–151.

31. Medvedev and Medvedev, p. 144.

CHAPTER SIX: A Tale of Two Sons

1. Archives of the Soviet Communist Party, RGANI, f. 89 (The Communist Party on Trial), op. 68, d. 1–7.

CHAPTER SEVEN: Relatives and Falsifying Death Certificates

1. APRF, f. 3, op. 58, d. 10, pp. 14–17, published in A. I. Kokurin and N. V. Petrov, editors, *Lubianka: Organy VChK-OGPU-NKVD-MGB-MVD-KGB. 1917–1991. Spravochnik* (Moskva: Mezhdunarodnyi Fond Demokratiia, 2003), Document No. 164, pp. 663–4,: Memo from S. D. Ignatiev to the Politburo "About the order of answering relatives of persons sentenced to death," October 30, 1951.

2. Archives of the Soviet Communist Party, RGANI, f. 89, op. 18, d. 35.

3. GARF, f. R-7523, op. 83, d. 4408, pp 8–9, published in *Istoriia Stalinskogo Gulaga,* Vol. 1, Document No. 225, p. 610. Statistical information of the Department for

the Preparation of Petitions for Pardoning under the Presidium of the Supreme Soviet of the USSR about the number of persons sentenced by special USSR courts (military tribunals, transport, and camp courts) in the period from 1940 to the first half of 1955.

4. *Istoriia Stalinskogo Gulaga,* Vol. 1, statistical appendix. pp. 608–645.
5. http://www.fsb.ru (publications).

CHAPTER EIGHT: The Ship of Philosophers

1. APRF, f. 3, op. 58, d. 175, pp. 1–2; 7–12, published in Khaustov et al, *Lubianka: Stalin i VChK-GPU-OGPU-NKVD. Ianvar' 1922–dekabr', 1936,* pp. 31–34.
2. RGASPI, f. 17, op. 3, d. 175, p. 31 and d. 304, p. 3, published in *Lubianka,* pp. 39–40.
3. APRF, f. 3, op. 58, d. 2, pp. 36–44, 46–58, published in *Lubianka,* pp. 52, 53.
4. RGASPI, f. 17, op. 3, d. 307, p. 2, published in *Lubianka,* p. 58.
5. APRF, f. 3, op. 58, d. 175, pp. 76–81, published in *Lubianka,* pp. 60–63.
6. Berdiaev's writings from exile published in Parisian émigré journals held in the Hoover Archives are summarized in David Satter, "The 'Russian Idea' of Nikolai Berdyaev," *Hoover Digest,* No. 4, Fall, 2006, pp. 236–242.
7. Vitalii Shetalinskii, "Oskolki serebrianogo veka," *Novy Mir,* 1998, Nos. 5–6.
8. Iurii Brodskii, *Solovki: Dvadtsat' let osobogo naznacheniia* (Moskva: Rosspen, 2002), pp. 472–4.
9. Archives of the Soviet Communist Party, f. 89 (Compiled by Lora Soroka) (Stanford: Hoover Institution Press, 2001), see entries under "Andropov."

CHAPTER NINE: Who Is the Prisoner Here?

1. Archives of the Soviet Communist Party, GARF, f. R-9414, op.1, d. 118, pp. 227a–232 (Hoover Institution Archives), published in *Istoriia Stalinskogo Gulaga,* Vol. 2, Document No. 187, pp. 451–3.
2. GARF, f. R-9414, op. 1, d. 895, pp. 27–30, published in *Istoriia Stalinskogo Gulaga,* Vol. 2, Document No. 137, pp. 279–281.
3. G. M. Ivanova, *Labor Camp Socialism: The Gulag in the Soviet Totalitarian System* (Armonk, N.Y.: M. E. Sharpe, 2000), p. 140, cited in Anne Applebaum, *Gulag: A History* (New York: Doubleday, 2003), p. 259.
4. Archives of the Soviet Communist Party, GARF, f. R-9414, op. 1, d. 947, pp. 191–194, published in *Istoriia Stalinskogo Gulaga,* Vol. 2, Document No. 155, p. 356.
5. TsAOPIM, f. 3352, op. 3, d. III, Volume 2, p. 8, cited in Oleg Khlevniuk, *The History of the Gulag* (New Haven: Yale University Press, 2004), p. 222.
6. G. M. Ivanova, *Labor Camp Socialism,* p. 160, cited in Applebaum, pp. 264–5.
7. GARF, f. R-9401, op. 1, d. 2244, pp. 373–4, published in *Istoriia Stalinskogo Gulaga,* Vol. 2, pp. 271–2.
8. G. M. Ivanova, *Labor Camp Socialism,* p. 163, cited in Applebaum, p. 261.

9. GARF, f. R-9401, op. 1, d. 2244, pp. 373–4 published in *Istoriia Stalinskogo Gulag*, Vol. 2, Document No. 132, p. 272.

10. GARF, f. R-9401, op. 1, d. 2244, p. 375, published in *Istoriia Stalinskogo Gulaga*, Vol. 2, Document No. 132, pp. 272–273.

11. Archives of the Soviet Communist Party, GARF, f. R-9414, op. 1, d. 2556, p. 10 (Hoover Institution Archives).

12. Archives of the Soviet Communist Party, GARF, f. R-9414, op. 1, d. 2552, p. 8.

13. Archives of the Soviet Communist Party, GARF, f. R-9414, op. 1, d. 2561, p. 29.

14. Archives of the Soviet Communist Party, GARF, f. R-9414, op. 1, d. 947, pp. 191–194, published in *Istoriia Stalinskogo Gulaga*, Vol. 2, Document No. 155, p. 357.

15. A. I. Kokurin and N. V. Petrov, compilers. *GULAG, 1918–1960 gg.* (Moskva, 2000, pp. 318, 320), cited in James Heinzen, "Corruption in the Gulag," in Leonid Borodkin, Paul Gregory, and Oleg Khlevnyuk, *Gulag: Ekonomika prinuditel'nogo truda* (Moskva: Rosspen, 2005), p. 169.

16. GARF, f. R-9401, op. 1, d. 499, pp. 1–4, published in *Istoriia Stalinskogo Gulaga*, Vol. 2, Document No. 61. Order of the NKVD USSR No. 00349 "About the militarized guarding of NKVD camps," June 5, 1938.

17. Archives of the Soviet Communist Party, GARF, f. R-9414, op. 1, d. 39, pp. 67a, 68–71, published in *Istoriia Stalinskogo Gulaga*, Vol. 4, Document No. 83, p. 197. Special communication of the deputy director of the operational department of the Gulag M. G. Kogenman to the deputy head of the Gulag G. S. Zavgorodnii "About the cohabitation of militarized guards in the Karagandinskii corrective labor camp with women; drunkenness and other violations of military discipline," October 22, 1941.

18. Archives of the Soviet Communist Party, GARF, f. R-9414, op. 1, d. 39, pp. 156–157, published in *Istoriia Stalinskogo Gulaga*, Vol. 4, Document No. 93, p. 216. Special communication of the head of the operational department of the Gulag Ia. A. Iorsh to the deputy minister of internal affairs S. N. Kruglov and the Gualg chief V. G. Nasedkin about the killing of two prisoners by an armed guard in the Yagrinskii corrective labor camp. June 30, 1942.

19. Archives of the Soviet Communist Party, GARF, f. R-9414, op. 1, d. 39, pp. 25–60, p. 5.

20. Archives of the Soviet Communist Party, GARF, f. R-9414, op. 1, d. 2552.

21. Applebaum, pp. 172–179, 272–3.

22. For documents on Gulag uprisings, see V. A. Kozlov and O. V. Lavinskaia (eds.), Vosstaniia, bunty i zabastovki zakliuchennykh in V. P. Kozlov (general editor), *Istoriia Stalinskogo Gulaga*, Vol. 6 (Moscow: Rosspen, 2004).

CHAPTER TEN: **Reasoning with Stalin on Zero Tolerance**

1. Decree of the Presidium of the Supreme Soviet of the USSR, "About criminal responsibility for theft of state or socialized property," June 4, 1947. Criminal Codex of the RSFSR. Moscow, 1950, pp. 142–143.

2. GARF, f. R-5446, op. 86a, d. 8073, pp. 3–12, published in *Istoriia Stalinskogo Gu-*

laga, Vol. 1, Document No. 205, pp. 564–568, "Report of the justice minister K. P. Gorshenin to I. V. Stalin about the execution of the decree of the Presidium of the Supreme Soviet 'About criminal responsibility for theft of state and socialized property of June 4, 1947' for the years 1947–1950," June 5, 1950.

3. Archives of the Soviet Communist Party, GARF, f. R-9474, op. 16, d. 368, pp. 91–93, published in *Istoriia Stalinskogo Gulaga,* Vol. 1, Document No. 206, pp. 568–570.

4. GARF, f. R-7523, op. 89, d. 4408, pp. 134–7, published in *Istoriia Stalinskogo Gulaga,* Vol. 1, Document No. 221, pp. 601–2. "Proposal of the Department for preparation of petitions for pardons for examination to the Presidium of the USSR Supreme Soviet regarding lowering the term of punishment of those sentenced according to the Decree of June 4, 1947.

CHAPTER ELEVEN: Bolshevik Discourse

1. *Politburo TsK RKP(b)-VKP(b): stenogrammy zasedanii, 1920–1930-e g.g.. V trekh tomakh,* Paul Gregory, Oleg Khlevniuk, and Aleksandr Vatlin, red. (Moskva: Rosspen, 2007).

2. Paul Gregory and Norman Naimark (eds.), *The Lost Transcripts of the Politburo* (New Haven: Yale University Press, forthcoming).

3. RGASPI, f. 17, op. 163, d. 700. Transcript of Combined Meeting of the Politburo of the Central Committee and the Presidium of the Central Control Commission, September 8, 1927 (Stenographic Report) "On the Internal Party Opposition."

4. RGASPI, f. 17, op. 163, d. 1011, pp. 211–215. "Combined meeting of the Politburo and the Presidium of the Central Control Commission on the Question of A. P. Smirnov, Eismont and others," November 27, 1932.

CHAPTER TWELVE: Invading Afghanistan

1. http://www.cnn.com/SPECIALS/cold.war/episodes/20/documents/brez.carter/.

2. G. F. Krivosheev, *Soviet Casualties and Combat Losses in the Twentieth Century* (London: Greenhill Books, 1993), pp. 285–289.

3. Archives of the Soviet Communist Party, RGANI, f. 89, op. 14, d. 24–41.

4. There is no Andropov document per se, but rather notes taken by Anatoly Dobrynin. See http://www.gwu.edu/~nsarchiv/NSAEBB/NSAEBB57/soviet.html.

5. Aleksandr Liakhovskii, *Tragediia i doblest' Afgana* (Moskva: GPI Iskon, 1995), pp. 109–112. Aleksandr Liakhovskii was a Major General, General Staff of the Russian Army. During the war in Afghanistan, he served as assistant to Commander of Operative Group of the USSR Defense Ministry in Afghanistan General V. I. Varennikov. The above excerpt was translated by Svetlana Savranskaya, the National Security Archive. See http://www.gwu.edu/~nsarchiv/NSAEBB/NSAEBB57/soviet .html.

6. http://www.departments.bucknell.edu/russian/const/77cons01.html#chap01.

7. Letter of Zbigniew Brzezinski to President Carter, December 26, 1979. See http:// www.gwu.edu/~nsarchiv/NSAEBB/NSAEBB57/soviet.html.

CHAPTER THIRTEEN: "Arbeit Macht Frei"

1. "Arbeit Macht Frei" ("Labor makes you free") was the sign above the main entrance to the Terezin concentration camp (among others) under the Nazis.
2. Archives of the Soviet Communist Party, RGANI, f. 89, op. 18, d. 36.
3. http://lcweb2.loc.gov/cgi-bin/query/r?frd/cstdy:@field(DOCID+ru0216).
4. These facts and figures are from Eugenia Belova and Paul Gregory, "Hang them All: The Economics of Crime and Punishment Under Stalin," A paper presented at the American Economic Association Meetings, Boston, January 2005.

CHAPTER FOURTEEN: Vladimir Moroz

1. Arkhiv UFSB po g. Moskva i Moskovskoi oblasti. Sledstvennoe delo Moroza Vladimira Grigor'evicha, pp. 1, 2, 6–10. 19–20, 23–24, 32–34, 45, 47–48, published in *Deti Gulaga, 1918–1956* (Mezhdunarodnyi Fond Demokratiia i Guverovskii institut: Moskva: Rosspen, 2002), pp. 283–293.

Abbreviations of Russian Archival Sources

TsAFSB	Central Archives of the Federal Security Service
RGASPI	Russian State Archives of Socio-Political History
APRF	Archives of the President of the Russian Federation
GARF	State Archives of the Russian Federation
RGANI	Russian State Archives of Contemporary History
TsAOPIM	Central Archives of Social and Political History of Moscow
Arkiv UFSB	Archives of the Directorate of the Federal Security Service

Illustration Source Notes

Chapter One

Photograph of the site of the Katyn massacre.

    CITATION: Jan Karski Collection, photographs, envelope S, Hoover Institution Archives.

Chapter Two

Photograph of Stalin with hunting comrades.
From photograph album, with title "Tov.Lakoba, sentiabr' 1933 g." documenting hunting trip including Stalin, Beriia, and others. Included in photo is Tukhachevsky, later executed on Stalin's orders.

    CITATION: Nestor Apollonovich Lakoba Collection, Hoover Institution Archives.

Chapter Three

Sketch of Lenin.

    CITATION: Artsybushev, IU. K. *"Diktatura proletariata" v Rossii. Nabroski s natury IU. K. Artsybusheva. Politicheskie dieiateli na zasiedlniiakh Sovietov rab., sold. i krest. deputatov, Uchreditel'nago sobraniia, krest'ianskikh s"iezdov i proch. V dekabrie 1917 i v ianvarie 1918 gg.* Moskva: Izd. T-va I. Knebel', [1918?], Hoover Institution Library.

Chapter Four

Painting by Vladimirov of a "former person."

    CITATION: Ivan Alekseevich Vladimirov Collection, Box 3, Hoover Institution Archives.

Chapter Five

Photograph of Nikolai Ezhov on top of Lenin Mausoleum, May 1, 1938.

    CITATION: Memorial Collection.

Chapter Six

Photograph of Yakov Dzhugashvili (Stalin's son) in German captivity.

    CITATION: World War II Pictorial Collection, Envelope FO, Hoover Institution Archives.

Chapter Seven

Photograph of Anna Akhmatova and her family.

    CITATION: Gleb Struve Collection, Envelope F, Hoover Institution Archives.

"Requiem" poem by Akhmatova, English translation.
> CITATION: Akhmatova, Anna. *The Akhmatova Journals, Volume I, 1938–41.* Edited by Lydia Chukovskaya; Poetry translated by Peter Norman. New York: Farrar, Straus & Giroux, 1994.

Portrait photograph of Anna Akhmatova.
> CITATION: Gleb Struve Collection, Envelope F, Hoover Institution Archives.

Chapter Eight

Poster of Lenin purging enemies.
> CITATION: Deni, V. N. "Tov.Lenin ochishchaet zemliu ot nechisti," poster, Hoover Institution Archives (Reprint. Original poster, 1920).

Chapter Ten

Detail of poster: Stalin with a group of collective farm workers.
> CITATION: Poster identification number RU/SU 1898, Poster Collection, Hoover Institution Archives.

Chapter Eleven

Sketches of (top) Trotsky, (center) Zinoviev, and (bottom) Kamenev.
> CITATION: Artsybushev, IU. K. *"Diktatura proletariata" v Rossii. Nabroski s natury IU. K. Artsybusheva. Politicheskie dieiateli na zasiedlniiakh Sovietov rab., sold. i krest. deputatov, Uchreditel'nago sobraniia, krest'ianskikh s"iezdov i proch. V dekabrie 1917 i v ianvarie 1918 gg.* Moskva: Izd. T-va I. Knebel', [1918?], Hoover Institution Library.

Chapter Twelve

Handwritten document with Politburo members' signatures authorizing Afghan war.
> CITATION: Hoover Institution Archives.

Chapter Fourteen

Photographic portrait of Stalin.
> CITATION: Noe Herrera Collection, Box 1, Hoover Institution Archives.

Index

concentration camps
Nazi, 154n1
Nazi *v.* Gulag, 90–91
confession
of Dzhugashvili, V., 67–69
of Enukidze, 55–56
Conquest, Robert, xii
conspiracies, 54–56
"Council of Social Activists," 87
crime(s)
criticism of Stalin as, 115–18
reporting, 101
of Stalin, 75
criminal justice system, 101
criminals, 50
repression of, 51–52
thieves as, 99–106

death
certificates, 74, 78
of Lenin, 24, 107
sentences, 20–22, 56
of Stalin, 60–61, 73, 90–91
democratic centralism, 81, 107
Democratic Republic of Afghanistan
(DRA), 120, 122
dictators, 23
dynasties of, 71
Hitler as, 20, 22
information and, 118
dictatorship, xi–xii
DRA. *See* Democratic Republic of Afghanistan
dynasty, 71–72
Dzerzhinskii, Feliks, 84, 89
Berdiaev on, 87
as head of secret police, 27
Dzhugashvili, Vasilii, 62–63
clemency denied for, 70–71
confession of, 67–69
military service of, 66
Dzhugashvili, Yakov, 62–63, *64*, 65–66

Eismont, N.B., 108, 115–18, 153n4
enemies
contingents of, 49–50
of Soviet Union, 48–49
of Stalin, 38, 46

Enukidze, A., 25
confession of, 55–56
Lenin's brain overseen by, 29
execution(s)
of Amin, 119, 123
family members to victims of, 73–76,
78
Great Terror, 20–22
NKVD, 3–4
planning, 6–7
of prisoners, 88
records of, 58–59
executioners, 22, 41
assembling, 1, 6
Great Terror, 60
Ezhov, Nikolai, 43, 45, *45*
family members and, 52–53
NKVD run by, 45, 47
record of executions ordered by, 59
simplified procedures allowed by,
54–56
terror plan by, 51

Falin, V., 10–11
family members, 140, 144–45
of Great Terror victims, 73–76, 78
as hostages, 52–53
sentence of, 74–76, 78, 150n1
Far North Construction, 17
former people, 37, *37*, 148n2
Lenin purging, *83*
punishing, 38–41
fraternization, 95–97
Free Academy of Religious Culture, 86
Frinovskii, M.P., 47, 59

Germany
Poland invaded by, 4–5
Soviet ambassador to, 30
Gestapo, 25, 65–66
Goebbels, Joseph, 3
Gorbachev, Mikhail, 4, 120
Afghanistan invasion and, 131–32
decision on revealing Katyn Massacre,
13–14
perestroika and, 9–11, 139
proposal from Soviet historians, 12
Gorshenin, K., 103

Soviet Union (*continued*)
collapse of, 74
Communist Party of, 128
enemies of, 48–49
military troops of, 122, 124, 132
Polish relations with, 10, 13
prison population of, 91
propaganda of, 129
repression in, 41
society, 36
as "worker–peasant state," 34–35
Stalin, Joseph, xi–xii, *16, 102, 143*
as absolute dictator, 118
administrators' relationships with,
102–5
Beria's memo to, 5–6
Central Committee and, 18–19
conspiracy to assassinate, 55–56
crimes of, 61, 75
criminal justice system of, 101
criticism of, 115–18
death of, 60–61, 73, 90–91
death sentences issued by, 20–22
enemies of, 38, 46
executions ordered by, 3–4
flattery utilized by, 19–20
Great Terror of, 43–46
Gulag camps after, 135–36
implications made by, 13–14
Lenin *v.,* 23–24
Lenin's brain and, 25
loyalists to, 107
as magnanimous, 16–18
orphans in regime of, 140–46
power and, 15, 72
sons of, 62–72
state security under, 135–36
successors of, 105–6
Trotsky *v.,* 109, *110,* 111–14
on Vogt, 28–29
Stenograms of the Politburo of the Communist Party, 108
Stetskii, A., 29–30

"Study of the Brain of V.I. Lenin," 31
Supreme Court of the USSR, 148n6

Taraki, 123
theft, zero-tolerance policy on, 99–106
Tolmachev, V.N., 115–18
totalitarianism, xi–xii
Tovstukha, Ivan, 24
Lenin's brain and, 26
troika
cases approved by, 55
chairman of, 58–59
compromise proposal submitted by,
104–5
in Great Terror, 46–47
punishing marginals/former
people, 40
sentences determined by, 78
simplified procedures of, 56–58
Trotsky, Leon, 34, 108
Stalin *v.,* 109, *110,* 111–14

United Nations, 131
United Opposition, 108
United States, 132–33
university students, 84
USSR Constitution, 128

Vietnam War, 132–33
Vogt, Oskar
attack on, 29–31
initial findings by, 31, 33
Lenin's brain studied by, 25, 26–29
Volin, A., 103, 105

Wegner, Gustav, 65
women, 96–97
work credit system, 137–38
World War II, 62, 93

zero-tolerance policy, 99–106
Zinovyev, Grigory, 108, *110,* 111–14

About the Author

PAUL R. GREGORY, a Hoover Institution research fellow, holds an endowed professorship in the Department of Economics at the University of Houston, Texas, and is a research professor at the German Institute for Economic Research in Berlin.

The holder of a Ph.D. in economics from Harvard University, he is the author or coauthor of twelve books and many articles on economic history, the Soviet economy, transition economies, comparative economics, and economic demography including *Lenin's Brain and Other Tales from the Secret Soviet Archives, The Political Economy of Stalinism* (2004), *Before Command: The Russian Economy from Emancipation to Stalin* (1994), *Restructuring the Soviet Economic Bureaucracy* (1990, reissued 2006), and *Russian National Income, 1885–1913* (1982, reissued 2005). He has edited *Behind the Façade of Stalin's Command Economy* (2001) and *The Economics of Forced Labor: The Soviet Gulag* (2003), both published by Hoover Press and summarizing his research group's work on the Soviet state and party archives. His publications based on work in the Hoover Archives have been awarded the Hewett Book Prize and the J. M. Montias Prize for the best article in the *Journal of Comparative Economics*. The research of his Hoover Soviet Archives Project team is summarized in part in "Allocation under Dictatorship: Research in Stalin's Archive" (coauthored with Hoover fellow Mark Harrison), published in the September 2007 issue of the *Journal of Economic Literature.*

Gregory also served on the editorial board of the seven-volume Gulag documentary series entitled *The History of the Stalin Gulag,* published jointly by the Hoover Institution and the Russian Archival Service. He is coordinating Hoover's Lost Politburo Stenogram Project and has edited a related book (with Hoover senior fellow Norman M. Naimark), *The Lost Transcripts of the Politburo* (forthcoming), and is involved in Hoover's ongoing acquisition of the Stalin Archive. He also serves or has served on the editorial boards of *Comparative Economic Studies, Slavic Review, Journal of Comparative Economics, Problems of Post-Communism,* and *Explorations in Economic History.*